SHE CAN KICK IT

The History of Women's Football Across the World via a Girl in Love with the Beautiful Game

Clare McEwen

She Can Kick It Press

Contents

Foreword

When Clare asked me to write the foreword of this book, I was delighted. I have had the pleasure of reading Clare's work each month for over two years and often look forward to her email dropping. Since she joined us as a features writer at *The Women's Football Magazine*, Clare has covered everything from the Barclays Women's Super League (WSL) and the Lionesses down to grassroots football, even writing about her own — often hilarious — experiences as a new coach.

With a passion for the game and a natural ability to tell the currently unknown stories, I was not surprised when I found out that Clare was planning on writing a book. Her own personal interest in learning more about the sport has led to discoveries of amazing untold tales which deserve to be heard from years gone by. With her own passion and the power in which she writes, there is nobody better to cover a history of the game.

There is no doubt that women's football has been on the rise in recent years, not just in its popularity but also in its changes of infrastructure, policies, and development, but how well do you know the history of our beautiful game?

Despite working in women's football for over eight years, I still love hearing about stories which can reignite my passion. If you look at the successes over recent years — the England Lionesses winning the 2022 European Championships, record attendances in the WSL and Barclays Championship, more young girls playing football at grassroots level than ever before — it can be easy to forget that there has been a real struggle to get to this point.

Clare's book delves into the history of not just the game in the United Kingdom but also across the whole world from unofficial championships to how the 1999 World Cup changed everything. Through Clare's charming, witty writing style and quotes from key figures throughout history, we can learn more about the women's game and just how many twists and turns there have been over the years.

You will come away from reading this book with a much richer understanding of why the game is the way it is now as well as having read some fantastic stories from people of all aspects of the game — I know I have. So, it's time to sit back, get a cup of tea and a biscuit and get ready to learn all the things you never knew you wanted to.

Helen Rowe-Willcocks

Founder, *The Women's Football Magazine*

Head of Women's Content, Manchester United

Introduction

The Girl in Love with the Beautiful Game

A tear traces its way down my wind-chapped face. I squeeze my son's gloved hand and try to answer his excited questions past the lump in my throat. The butterflies in my stomach threaten to burst out and swoosh past the person beside me. A gentle ripple of noise spreads as people shuffle and sit. The crowd grows. So does the excitement. Another tear steers down my cheek and plops onto the newly bought scarf around my neck. I try to hold in the well of emotion trying to burst through the shaky dam.

I open the programme for distraction and point out the players to my young son. A smile broadens across my face as I let the images sink in. The noise increases. More hustle, more bustle. People find their seats.

It's November 2019. This is my first visit to Wembley Stadium.

We're a long way up as we look onto the crisp, green grass and immaculate white lines below. Time ticks on. I fidget, trying to hold back the wave of excitement as it bubbles up inside me. But it's no good. I grin from ear to ear as tears stream down my face. The players jog onto the pitch below.

It's five years since the Lionesses last played at the home of football, and this time they've pulled in a record crowd of 77,768 people, all here to watch them take on Germany in a friendly. The 10-year-old me, wrapped in a 40-something- year-old body, is bursting with pride, excitement, and disbelief because back in the mid-1980s, the actual 10-year-old me could never have dreamt of this moment: watching women run out onto the hallowed turf of Wembley — literally, the stuff of dreams.

Since that evening at Wembley, I've been to two Women's FA Cup Finals there, including watching my beloved Manchester United Women lift the trophy. Despite living hundreds of miles away, I've followed United to Old Trafford and Leigh Sports Village. I've been to a Euros match at Milton Keynes, I've watched the Lionesses beat the U.S. on their first visit back to Wembley after that historic Euro 2022 win, and I've watched them win the first Finalissima on penalties. Each time, the tears — filled with pride and joy — escape my leaky eyes. But as I wipe them away, I see today's 10-year-old girls proudly wearing their replica kits, the names of their idols emblazoned across their backs: Russo, Toone, Daly, Williamson, Earps. Today, proud dads take their girls to games and wait with them to get treasured autographs and selfies with their idols; they find opportunities for their daughters to play and speak highly of the stars on the pitch.

I think I have something in my eye again.

Although he never got the chance, I think my dad would have fully supported my football dream, too, if society had allowed me to follow it. My dad introduced me to football, albeit accidentally, as he shouted at the players on TV each weekend. Across our small living room, I listened, watched, learned, and fell in love with the beautiful game.

Rewind to 1985. It's my 10th birthday. I'm excited about my disco party later, but first, presents. I rip off the coloured wrapping, wide-eyed and big-smiled, as I realise what this one is: my very first proper football. The white globe gleams: it's the most beautiful thing I've ever touched. I rip open the next present and can't believe my newly 10-year-old eyes. A shiny pair of black football boots stare back at me; their two magical white stripes and smattering of studs symbolise I'm a footballer (two stripes rather than three because we couldn't afford Adidas).

My dad bought me that football. At a time when girls rarely played, at a time when we were called tomboys, my dad went to his mate's sports shop and bought me a football. In the 1980s. Until recently, I hadn't considered how big a deal that was. I wish I'd thought to thank him. (I'll thank my mum, she probably had to nag him a lot anyway.)

I tug on my birthday boots, grab my shiny new ball, and head to the park. My mates are there, mostly boys, jumpers for goalposts, and a quick game of headers and volleys. It's my Wembley. I wheel away after a close-range volley hits the back of the imaginary net. This is my best life. Playing football. I play in the playground; the boys have deemed me "good enough" to join in. I play in our small garden, although I spend as much time hopping the wall to retrieve the ball as kicking it. I play in our hallway, driving my mum mad. I'm obsessed.

In the '80s, that was what football was for a girl living in a quiet Cornish town — there were no teams for girls. I watched as my male friends went off for their Saturday afternoon matches, wistfully imagining what it would be like. I tried to emulate it. I created my own team — Girls United. My mates and I met at 3 pm every Saturday. It soon fizzled out, maybe because of my slight megalomania: captain, player-manager, all-controlling football monster. Nah, they just weren't as obsessed as me.

I wonder what could have happened if I'd pushed harder against the status quo.

Such a contrast with now. Ten minutes' walk from where I volleyed my first ball into an imaginary top corner, Helston Athletic Women's team is doing it for real. They've celebrated goals on the same pitch where I'd longingly watched my male mates play.

I've continued to watch football all my life, but being part of a football team has mostly eluded me. I played my only competitive match at university before an ongoing injury stopped me.

At least, that was the story until I became a mum.

My son has inherited my love of football and enabled me to get back into it. We've spent countless hours kicking a ball around the back garden (it substituted for a school run during lockdown when we were homeschooling). I played with him and his mates at the park. I helped run an after-school club, coached the school team, and now I'm the manager of his under-13s team. We follow the game together, women's and men's. I write features for The Women's Football Magazine. I'm part of football again.

So now feels the right time to put my 25 years of academic research experience into writing the story of women's football and sharing how women battled against the odds to bring the game to where it is today. In my own small way, by coaching a youth team in a male-dominated space and by writing this book, I hope I'm pushing the narrative forward just a little bit — something I couldn't do when I was 10.

But this book isn't about me. It's about all the players who have continued to push hard against the barriers, who've sacrificed, and who didn't take "no" for an answer. It's about the trailblazers and the pioneers. It's about those who forged a path so that today's players can stand on their shoulders and elevate the game to dizzying new heights.

Have you ever wondered about the identities of these women or the reasons behind the 50-year ban on their game? Want to know how women kicked their way from being actively sabotaged to globally celebrated? Are you curious about the pioneers who blazed through the obstacles and the men who helped them by challenging their peers? Then this book is for you.

Come on a journey through time with this light-hearted look at how women's football has progressed across the world from the 19th century until now. Meet the individuals who made a difference. Experience the rise of the game as it spreads in popularity, overcoming prejudices and building resilience into the very fabric of the sport.

I dedicate this book to all the 10-year-old girls who ever wanted to play but couldn't. To all the 10-year-old girls who did play and pushed our game forward. And to all the 10- year-old girls, now and in the future, who get to live out their footballing dreams.

Standing on the shoulders of giants.

I also dedicate this book to my Mum, Dad, sister Nicola, and Auntie Max, who never questioned my love of football; my husband Hamish, who endures it; and my son Jamie, who reignited my passion.

1

The Early Years

There is evidence of women playing football for as long as there is evidence of football. Shakespeare talks about it in A Comedy of Errors in 1594. The National Football Museum in Manchester has the following quote displayed, which records a conversation between two shepherds talking about women playing football in 1580:

"A tyme there is for all, my mother often sayes, when she, with skirts tuckt very hy, with girls at football playes".

There are church documents dating back to 1628 that record instances of women playing football in Lanarkshire, Scotland, and there are accounts of fisherwomen playing an annual match in Scotland in the late 18th century. Football has been played and enjoyed for centuries by both men and women.

Modern football, as we know it, began in Britain in the 19th century. There was an attempt to formalise the rules at the University of Cambridge in 1843, but it wasn't until 1863 that a printed set of rules was first produced, and the English Football Association was formed.

Men and women played the sport in teams all over the world, and everybody lived happily ever after. The end. Wouldn't that have been nice?

Well, it pretty much was for men, but for women, the story is a bit more of a struggle. It's a tale of determination, resilience, individual bravery, mass resistance, more resilience, and very slow progress.

To appreciate where football is now for women, you need to know the journey it took to get there. The story in England provides the backbone of this history, but gradually, the beautiful game spread throughout the world, sweeping up women from all corners of the Earth into its orbit. The story goes something like this.

Once the rules of the game were established, football grew. Alongside more men's teams, women tried to form teams and leagues. But society demanded women fit into the roles and ideals set out by men, and football was regarded as a whim of wealthy women, not something to be taken seriously.

Despite the attitudes of the time, the earliest recorded international football match between women was Scotland versus England, played in Edinburgh in May 1881. On May 7th at Hibernian Park, Edinburgh, teams from London and Glasgow competed in what is described as the first international. The game ended with Scotland winning 3-0. Lily St Clair scored the opener and became the first recorded female goalscorer. This match was played less than 10 years after the first international men's match in 1872. Women's and men's football might be at a similar level today if attitudes towards women had been different.

After this first international, a report in the   laid the foundation for how women footballers would be described for many years to come. They were described not by their skill and determination but by their clothes and appearance. The report included put-downs and scathing comments to make sure the women didn't get ideas above their station: football was a man's game.

Despite the negative attitudes from the press and certain sections of society, the first documented international seemed to have been generally well received and went off without incident. Unfortunately, the same couldn't be said of the next game. According to newspaper reports at the time, the next match was played in Glasgow in front of several thousand spectators. During the match, a few hundred men invaded the pitch and harassed the players. The match had to be abandoned, and the players ushered to safety. There were chaotic scenes of vandalism and fighting between spectators and police, and players had to escape in a horse-drawn bus. Undeterred, the men threw items at the vehicle as it was leaving.

Several years later, in April 1887, a letter was sent to the *Wakefield and West Riding Herald* newspaper about a local match between women. The letter writer wrote:

"The sight of women so far unsexing themselves as publicly to wear the dress of men and play a game we are accustomed to regards as a purely masculine sport, is not easily reconcilable with our ideas of the fitness of things".

These two episodes, a violent pitch invasion and a letter rant, show the sexist attitudes of the time and what the women were up against. People had already decided that football wasn't a game for women, so they put an end to it with their jeers, violence, and ideas of superiority.

Well, they tried. Many of them kept on trying for the next 100-plus years. Some are still trying. But only a few days after the display of hooliganism at the Scotland versus England match in Glasgow, the women were back on the pitch in another international friendly. This time, there was no repeat of the violent reaction seen in Glasgow, and the tour moved safely to England.

Some matches were successful, and others ended in pitch invasions. Whatever happened, the women continued to play.

It wasn't long before local clubs formed. The British Ladies' Football Club was one of the first. It began in 1895, under the guidance of Alfred Hewitt Smith and their player-captain-secretary, Nettie Honeyball.

Nettie wanted to play football, so in 1894, she placed an advert in her local newspaper asking other women to join her. Around 30 women answered and came to train, which showed the level of enthusiasm even in the strict Victorian era. Given the political and cultural climate of the time, getting 30 local women playing football together was a big deal. Like the world, Britain was run by men, and although educated women were talking about equal rights, women getting the same voting rights as men was still decades away (not until 1928). Nettie and her Honeyballers were determined to change the football landscape.

The aristocrat Lady Florence Dixie, a woman's rights advocate and fan of sport, became their patron, giving them some financial backing. Lady Florence always worked hard to match her brothers physically in sport and understood why the women wanted to play. She became a key figure in the movement, organising matches and becoming the president of the British Ladies' FC team.

Victorian Britain, with its strict rules and expectations, disapproved of women playing a "man's game", though. To stop them, medical professionals were asked for their opinions on how the sport might affect a woman's body, and they concluded that playing was unsafe because their bodies were needed for childbearing. A report from the British Medical Association at the time said,

"It is impossible to think of what happens when the arms are thrown up to catch the ball, or when a kick is made with full force, and misses, without admitting the injury which may be thereby produced in the inner mechanism of the female frame. Not can one overlook the chances of injury to breasts… in regard to the proper use of the breast, however, in the rearing of infants, there can be no doubt of the deleterious influences".

Many encouraged the ban to prevent women from playing on health grounds, but there was no evidence to support the wild claims that sport would harm women's reproductive health or cause infertility. No evidence, just a will to whip up some opposition against women playing football.

Fortunately, the newly formed British Ladies' FC were undeterred and continued to train regularly. Local male players coached them, including Tottenham Hotspur's centre-half, J.W. Julian, an early male advocate. With twice weekly practice, the football of the British Ladies' team improved, and in March 1895, they were ready for their first game. Because there weren't any local competitors, the club was divided into two teams, a "North" team and a "South" team, to enable them to play a match against each other. You might need to sit down for this. Ten thousand people came out to watch that first game in Crouch End, London, and thousands more were turned away.

Nettie Honeyball was not the actual name of the founder of the British Ladies', but a pseudonym (it's thought her real name was Mary Hutson). Not much is known about this enigmatic woman, but she had a passion for football and a fighting spirit. When asked why she was trying to start a football team, she replied,

"Why not? Aren't women as good as men? We ladies have too long borne the degradation of presumed inferiority to the other sex. The subject has been in my mind for years. If men can play football, so can women."

An interview published in *The Sketch* on the 6th of February 1895 reinforced her sentiments:

"I founded the association late last year, with the fixed resolve of proving to the world that women are not the 'ornamental and useless' creatures men have pictured. I must confess, my convictions on all matters, where the sexes are so widely divided, are all on the side of emancipation and I look forward to the time when ladies may sit in Parliament and have a voice in the direction of affairs, especially those which concern them most."

Nettie was a Victorian-age badass, and she wasn't the only one. Another member of the British Ladies' team was Scottish suffragette Helen Matthew. She was a keen footballer, and there are reports she played before joining Nettie's team. Playing under the pseudonym "Mrs Graham", she played in goal.

After the Crouch End match between the North and South teams, the British Ladies' Football Club went on tour and played throughout the country as the North and South teams, spreading the word about football. In April 1895, they played in a charity event, the Festival of Football in Brighton. The event raised money for local medical charities, and 5,000 people came to watch them. The games continued up and down the country, as did the newspaper reports that mostly focused on what the women were wearing and criticising them.

When the football season restarted after a summer break, there had been a change within the British Ladies'. Mrs Graham had left the team and formed a rival team known as Mrs Graham's XI. She took many of the players with her, and for a while, both teams claimed to be the "Original Lady Footballers". They both played North versus South matches all over the country, including in Wales and Scotland. Since both teams now claimed to be the originals and both teams were using Lady Florence Dixie's name, the aristocrat withdrew her support and her money. The teams continued to travel around the British Isles promoting the game, but without Lady Florence's financial backing, they struggled, and a few years later, both teams disbanded. The interest in women playing football faded away for a while.

About 20 years later, the First World War changed everything. Whilst men were on the front lines, risking their lives for their country, women took up all the roles in society they had vacated. Many women became factory workers, and it is here that our story continues.

Many factories were in the north of England and Scotland, and football became popular with the female factory workers. During their work breaks, they would kick a ball around to relax, and soon, teams formed so they could play competitive matches. Since the Football Association (FA) was forced to suspend the men's league now their players were at war, there was a natural gap in the market. It was good for morale to have matches to distract people, and local interest grew. The teams often had men coaching and training them, and with the FA's support, they began playing fixtures at local grounds.

Women from different factories got a chance to play competitive football, and whilst they did, they raised funds for the war effort from ticket sales. Money raised went to charities that supported injured soldiers, and the appetite was so great that matches often drew crowds of tens of thousands of spectators.

Undoubtedly, the most famous of these factory teams was Dick, Kerr Ladies, who formed in 1917 — one of the first organised factory teams — and continued for 48 years until 1965. During that time, they played 833 games, winning the vast majority. They began in Preston, Lancashire, forming at Dick, Kerr & Co., a tram building and light railway works. During World War I, the facility became a munitions factory. Dick, Kerr Ladies showed their early potential when they beat a team of men at the factory. Alfred Frankland, an office worker, watched the game from his office and, being something of a visionary, saw potential and began to organise the team. He arranged matches, pitches, and gave them structure and direction — he became Dick, Kerr Ladies manager.

Up and down the country, factory teams of women formed. They played regular charity matches and raised money from ticket sales to help injured servicemen: a noble cause that people supported. And people supported in numbers. Their first game was a Christmas Day fixture against another local team, Arundel Coulthard Foundry. The match was played at Deepdale, Preston North End's ground, and drew a crowd of around 10,000 people. It raised £600, over £50,000 in modern money. There are reports of other matches drawing crowds of 55,000 spectators — the matches were popular.

Frankland continued to grow and improve his team, and they became dominant in England. So, he decided to go international. He arranged a game against a French team in the spring of 1920, billing it England vs France. The English team was represented by Dick, Kerr Ladies, and the French team was represented by

their French equivalent, Fémina Sport. The game drew a crowd
of 25,000 spectators to Deepdale. In the autumn of the same year,
the Dick, Kerr Ladies became the first team to play overseas when
they played the return fixture in France. The two teams toured the
country, playing matches against each other.

Profile: Lily Parr

Lily Parr stood out as the biggest star of the Dick, Kerr Ladies (and
probably the best player of her generation). She was also a goal-
scoring machine. Born in St Helens, England, in 1905, Lily was only 15
when she began to stand out and was a player often picked out by the
media for her "skilful and clever style". Lily scored with alarming
regularity and totalled around 1000 goals during her 30-year career. In
2002, she was the first woman to be inducted into the National
Football Museum's Hall of Fame and in 2019, a statue of her was
unveiled at the museum.

The Dick, Kerr Ladies returned home unbeaten and were
welcomed back by crowds of fans cheering them on. Throughout
the 1920s, the two teams played many times in both England and
France. Dick, Kerr Ladies continued to thrive and helped draw a
crowd of 53,000 when they played St Helens Ladies at Goodison
Park on Boxing Day, 1920. They were at the height of their fame
in 1921 and often played two games a week at grounds all over
the country. During that year, they played around 60 matches,
playing in front of around 900,000 people, and all of this whilst
still working full-time at the factory.

By this time, of course, the war had ended, and men were back playing football. The Dick, Kerr Ladies and their counterparts from other factory teams had become very successful during the time the men were away. Unfortunately, this became the downfall of the sport they loved.

The popularity of women's games meant they were taking fans away from the men's game, and the authorities were getting uneasy about it. Women's matches were now in direct competition with men's matches. The FA began to dismantle the reputation of the teams and accused them of stealing the money they'd raised for charity. There is no evidence to support these claims. Even if there was any wrongdoing around the charitable money, the women were not the ones responsible for the finances, the male managers were. The women only received minimal expenses. Even without evidence, the rumours and speculation were enough for the FA to help justify their next move. In December 1921, the FA decided to put a stop to women playing and, under the claims that football "was an unsuitable game for women", they banned them from playing on Football Association (FA) affiliated pitches. Since the FA had control of most of the pitches, this was considered a complete ban on the game for women in England. The ban was in place for 50 years.

Under the ban, although women's teams could form, they found it very difficult to find anywhere to train and play. Teams ended up playing in parks, on rugby and cricket pitches, or on scraps of land, relying on non-FA landowners to allow them to play. Dick, Kerr Ladies escaped this restriction because they were in the fortunate position of owning their own pitch. Showing remarkable forethought, the Dick, Kerr company had bought Ashton Park for them to play on in 1919, so their pitch wasn't under the control of the FA. They continued to play and train pretty much as they had before the ban. Except now they wanted to spread the word that women played football. In 1922, they took the team global and toured Canada and the United States of America.

Unfortunately, when they arrived in Canada, they found out the local football association had banned them from playing in their country too, as the English FA ban spread throughout the Commonwealth. When they moved on to the USA, they discovered there were no women's teams for them to play against. The team was devastated, but they played men's teams to avoid a wasted trip. Their tour lasted nine weeks, and they played nine games: won 3, drew 3, and lost 3. Not bad for a bunch of women playing a sport not suitable for their delicate bodies. Undeterred, they continued to make history at home too when in 1923 they played the first ever match at night under electric lights. Their opponents for the game at Turf Moor cricket ground, Burnley, were Hey's Ladies of Bradford.

Despite continuing to be known as Dick, Kerr Ladies, they officially changed their name to Preston Ladies in 1926. In 1957 their manager Alfred Frankland died, and Kath Latham took over until they disbanded because of a lack of players in 1965. During their 48-year history, they raised large sums of money for charity, somewhere around £180,000 according to the research of Gail

Newsham — an expert on Dick, Kerr Ladies. This is equivalent to over £10 million in today's money. They attracted crowds as large as 50,000 spectators and, along with other factory teams in England, and France's Fémina Sport, they helped spread the joy of football to other women. They are the most famous women's team from the game's early history, a reputation they deserve since they worked tirelessly to raise both money and the game's profile. Without Dick, Kerr Ladies and Alfred Frankland, the developing story of women's football would be very different. But what was happening throughout the rest of Europe?

2

The 1920s-1930s: The Rise and Fall

The Rest of the British Isles

As we saw early in the previous chapter, women were playing football in Scotland in the 1880s. Not only playing but winning, since Scotland won the first meeting of their international rivalry with England. As far as is currently known, Scotland's early history mostly mirrored that of their English counterparts, but detailed information is still lacking.

The first women's match in Scotland to be played under the Scottish Football Association's (SFA) guidelines took place at Shawfield Grounds, Rutherglen, near Glasgow, in 1892, although the SFA did not support it. A few years later, the British Ladies' Football Club toured Scotland, bringing with it publicity and possibility and no doubt inspiring the formation of more Scottish women's teams. The press and authorities dismissed women's football as a novelty just as they did south of the border, but as in England, factory teams of women formed all over the country as the war began. Many matches were played in front of large crowds, and as more and more teams appeared, spectators came out to watch. A lot of money was raised for charities in Scotland, as it was in England. But just as women's football quickly rose with the outbreak of war, when the men came back home, it was expected to disappear, and women were expected to quietly go back to fulfilling their roles as wives and mothers, not enjoy sport. The Scottish Football Association (SFA) didn't formally ban women from playing like the English FA did. Instead, they placed similar restrictions on playing, effectively banning it without officially banning it. Whatever the reason behind this, it wasn't because they in any way supported women playing football.

Rutherglen Ladies in Scotland, like the Dick, Kerr Ladies in England, weren't put off by the restrictions, and the team became legendary in Scotland. Formed near Glasgow in 1921, Rutherglen founder and manager James H. Kelly had similar plans to his English counterpart, Alfred Frankland: to promote the game. Kelly quickly built his team, and by 1922, they regularly played local men's teams and brought in crowds of spectators. Alfred Franklin, at the time, had proclaimed Dick, Kerr Ladies as "World Champions" because of their formidable record against other teams. James Kelly was quick to respond and said they couldn't be World Champions if they hadn't yet played and beaten his Rutherglen Ladies. Game on. The two teams met in 1923, and on this occasion, James Kelly was right to be cocky as Rutherglen Ladies snatched the crown from Dick Kerr with a 2-0 victory. Rutherglen were now "World Champions". Over the years, the crown of "World Champion" passed back and forth between the two teams, but Dick, Kerr Ladies held the title for most of their rivalry.

Dick, Kerr's stand-out player was often Lily Parr (a superstar of her time). For Rutherglen, it was their captain, Sadie Smith (side note: whose granddaughter is folk singer Eddi Reader). Molly Seaton was another of Rutherglen's stars. Kelly had brought "Big Molly" in from Ireland to help them beat their English rivals. Molly was Belfast's best player before Kelly brought her to join his "Scotland" team to get one over on England. If nothing else, this shows how seriously football was taken by those inside the game, even in the 1920s.

Many successful years followed for Rutherglen Ladies, but they disbanded in 1939 and passed the baton on to the newly formed Edinburgh Ladies, who picked up where Rutherglen left off and began playing high-profile games against men's teams in the late 1930s. In 1937, Edinburgh Ladies played Dick, Kerr Ladies in the "Championship of the World" match. The game at Squires Gate, Blackpool, finished with the English side winning 5-1, but Edinburgh were just getting into their stride. By 1939 Edinburgh was beating virtually every other women's team in Scotland, so they took on the mighty Dick, Kerr Ladies again. This time the game was in Scotland and Edinburgh won to become "World Champions". They didn't keep the title for long as a few weeks later, they had to give it back to Dick, Kerr Ladies again. The timing of Edinburgh Ladies' rise was unfortunate, though, as World War II soon interrupted the growth of women's football.

Football in Wales started slowly, probably because the Welsh national sport is rugby, but the British Ladies' team helped spread the word of the beautiful game across the border from England. Thousands of people came out to watch their games, and more Welsh teams formed, inspired by seeing other women play. Early on, some of the women's teams played men's teams. There's a report of one of these games inspiring the girls in Pontypool enough for them to ask a local butcher for a bladder that they could turn into a ball [author's note: it brings me great joy to think of these young girls so eager to play that they found a substitute ball in a butcher's shop]. Despite this flurry of excitement, though, women's football fizzled out in Wales for a few years. During World War I, there was a resurgence as teams formed in factories and matches raised money for charity. During the 1920s and 1930s, Dick, Kerr Ladies toured Wales and played games against teams such as Cardiff and Swansea. Unable to play on football pitches because of the ban, they played on rugby pitches instead (plentiful in Wales). In 1921, 18,000 people watched a game at Cardiff Arms Park. Wherever women played, crowds gathered. Soon, objections on religious grounds bubbled up, and Football Association Wales (FAW) introduced their ban in 1922.

A British Ladies' tour in 1895 introduced football to women in Northern Ireland, but the first major rise in participation came during the First World War. In 1921, ten thousand people watched a match between Ireland and England at Windsor Park. The game was a testimonial in honour of Mrs Walter Scott, who was considered a pioneer of women's football in Ireland because she organised matches to raise money for charity. Four years before this testimonial, Mrs Scott had organised her first match, a game set up to raise money for charity. Despite being instrumental in organising football in her country, her first name was never documented in football articles: she was always referred to as Mrs Walter Scott. This shows how society viewed women at the time as wives, not individuals. Despite this, Mrs Scott clearly had her own ideas and, in 1916, set up the Ladies Football Guild in her home country. It was Irish born "Big Molly" Seaton who sparked broader interest when, as part of Rutherglen, she toured Northern Ireland in 1927. Molly was a centre-back, a corner taker, a goalscorer, and an all-round footballing legend. Her skill and fame meant she could draw a crowd, and she's still considered one of the best players produced by Ireland. Very well aware of her worth, Molly often charged a fee for playing and even had her own agent at one point. Definitely ahead of her time. It was Molly and the Rutherglen Ladies who played the first big game in the Republic of Ireland (then known as the Irish Free State) too, when they played in front of 12,000 spectators in Dublin in 1927. Molly scored seven goals against a local Irish team. I hope she was being paid a goal bonus.

Mainland Europe

France was at a similar stage to England by 1920. But unlike the factory teams from England, the French women's teams were born out of sports clubs. These clubs often ran various teams in different sports and included accomplished high school and university athletes. Two of the more successful teams to be founded at such clubs were Fémina Sport and En Avant. Fémina

Sport was formed in Paris in 1912, and since they were the first club around, they played matches amongst themselves or against local schoolboy teams. Soon, other sports clubs were keen to get involved, and after seeing a Fémina Sport match, representatives of the En Avant sports club formed their own women's football team.

Organised women's football began in France in 1917 when the Fédération des Sociétés Féminines Sportives de France (FSFSF) formed, helped by Alice Milliat — a keen women's sport activist. In 1919, Alice became a driving force for the game in her country when she became president of the FSFSF and organised the first French women's football championship. Alice wasn't just an advocate for football for women but for all women's sport. A keen athlete, she played various sports and was a member of the Fémina Sport Club. In 1919, she asked the International Association of Athletics Federations (IAAF) to allow women to compete in track and field events at the 1924 Olympics. They refused. So, she helped organise the 1921 Women's World Games, also known as the 1921 Women's Olympiad: the first international women's multi-sports event. In 1920, she led the Fémina Sport women's football team to England to play against Dick, Kerr Ladies.

In a 1934 interview, Alice said:

"Women's sports of all kinds are handicapped in my country by the lack of playing space. As we have no vote, we cannot make our needs publicly felt, or bring pressure to bear in the right quarters. I always tell my girls that the vote is one of the things they will have to work for if France is to keep its place with the other nations in the realm of feminine sport."

Despite Alice's best efforts, the sport was slow to catch on, and the first FSFSF tournament in 1919 featured only Fémina Sport and En Avent. Fémina Sport, in particular, was a club very much ahead of its time, and in 1919 they had an all-female management staff. They were the dominating club in France in the 1920s, the French equivalent of Dick, Kerr in England and Rutherglen in Scotland. Their most famous player was Carmen Pomiès, who was part of the team that toured England. She became friends with Dick, Kerr Ladies' Florrie Redford, and after Fémina Sport's first tour, she stayed in England to play alongside Florrie at Dick, Kerr Ladies. Carmen Pomiès toured the United States (U.S.) with Dick, Kerr in 1922 before going back to France, joined for a while by Florrie Redford. Pomiès became captain of Fémina Sport and later France.

The rivalry between Fémina Sport (billed as France) and Dick, Kerr Ladies (billed as England) and their regular tours on either side of the channel helped keep women's football bubbling away in Europe. Like Dick Kerr, Ladies, Fémina Sport had their own ground — Stade Elisabeth — which made it easier to find somewhere to play. Fémina Sport, playing as France, also regularly played Belgium's national team, and the last match this France team played was against Belgium in 1932. It was the last match because, in 1933, the French Football Federation (FFF) banned women from playing.

Bans spread throughout Europe as football federations began citing similar reasons to the English FA to stop women playing, "it's an unsuitable game for women". Having grown beyond the original two teams, the French women's championship stopped. It had run continuously from its establishment in 1919 until the ban in 1933.

As you've just read, women played football in Belgium too, and in 1923, the women's football federation, Féderation Sportive Féminin Belge, organised their first domestic championship. But it was the international games against France that sparked the most interest. In 1924, Belgium and France met for their first international. Since women in Belgium were also banned from male pitches, the game ended up being played in an indoor velodrome. If you're not familiar, a velodrome is a sporting arena for track cycling, the one with banked sides and a small space in the middle. The match was played in that small space in the middle. It had grass laid on it rather than the hard wooden floors you see at modern velodromes, but still. Over 1,200 people crammed into the venue to watch. As well as being the first international match between these two teams, it was also the first indoor international. A return match in France was played in front of 5,000 people on an actual football pitch. Throughout the 1920s, games continued in Belgium. In the middle of the decade, two domestic teams, Brussels Fémina and Atalente, toured Portugal and Spain. Nine teams competed in a national championship during the decade, but by 1933, the domestic league had dwindled, and the growth of women's football in Belgium stalled.

In Austria, too, matches began in earnest, and in 1923, a weekly newspaper called for women interested in playing football to let them know. Hundreds of women wrote back, and the following year, 50 women passed a medical check and met for their first training session. Clubs formed, but after this brief flurry of activity, there was a decade-long period where few matches took place. In 1934, Edith Klinger took matters into her own hands and founded the club Kolossal, later named 1. Winer D.F.C. (1. Viennese Ladies Football Club). Soon after, she asked interested women to contact her; by 1935, they got together for their first training session. A breakaway group formed a second club, and Klinger became an officially qualified referee, the first female referee in Austria. By early 1936, representatives from several Austrian teams met to discuss founding a women's football association. The Österreichische Damenfußball Union (ÖDU — Austrian Ladies Football Union) was approved a few months later. Of course, the men's football federation got twitchy about the rise in popularity and banned them from their pitches. The women carried on regardless and formed a championship in 1937.

In Germany, there is evidence that women played football at the turn of the 18th Century, and in the 1920s, there were students' matches at the German University Championships. But stories in Germany were similar to those throughout Europe and women playing football were met with disapproval. Undeterred, one young woman put pen to paper and wrote an advertisement in a newspaper to find like-minded women to play. Lotte Specht was 18 years old when she wrote her advert in March 1930, and soon, 35 women had replied. Later that year, Lotte founded the 1st Deutscher Damen Fußballclub (DDFC) in Frankfurt. The team split into two to play matches (since they were the only team around) but were generally met with hostility and disapproval. In fact, with pressures from society and their parents, gradually, the young players quit their hobby, and by the autumn of 1931, the club was no more. Another example of young women's football dreams being destroyed. The Deutscher Fußball- Bund (DFB) (German Football Federation) imposed a ban in 1936.

In Spain, a women's football association was formed in Valencia in 1932, which enabled local teams to play against each other. The association sponsored four teams — Levante, España, Valencia, Atlético — and they toured their home country and Latin America, spreading the joy of football through the Spanish-speaking world. In Barcelona, the multi-sports club Club Femení i d'Esports de Barcelona showed cultural progress when Ana María Martínez Sagi was the first woman appointed to the board of directors to advocate for women's sport. But just as there were signs of progress, the Spanish Civil War began. The resulting Franco dictatorship, which continued until 1975, banned women from playing football. Despite the risks involved, it didn't stop everyone, but it wasn't until the 1970s that women's football grew again in Spain.

Although organised women's football didn't begin in the Nordic countries until the 1960s, Norway had a unique introduction when, in 1928, a match featuring Norwegian superstar Sonja Henie took place. Sonja was a celebrated figure skater and had won three Olympic titles, 10 World titles, and six European titles before becoming a glamorous film star. When she turned her feet to football, she brought her fanbase. Unusually, but perhaps

understandably, given Sonja's previous exploits, the early matches
she took part in were decided on style points rather than the
number of goals scored. Make of that what you will.

The Rest of the World

I must confess that when I started researching Australia's football
history, I wasn't expecting to find much — I assumed it was
a relatively new sport Down Under. I was wrong. The first
public match between two women's teams was played when
North Brisbane (the "Reds") beat South Brisbane (the "Blues")
in 1921. Although there had been previous reports of games,
this is considered the first properly documented women's match
in Australia. Maybe because it was played in front of 10,000
spectators — yep, women's football started big in Australia.
Despite being on the other side of the globe, Australia was not
out of reach of the FA ban in England. Since they were then
part of the Commonwealth, there was a strong English influence,
and public opinion in Australia swayed towards the English FA's
stance. An Australian committee agreed that women's bodies
weren't suitable, and (surprise) it was banned. In New Zealand,
during the First World War period, matches were played to raise
money for charity. There were clubs in Auckland, Wellington, and
Christchurch, but again, it was quickly banned.

China's history is unique, but ultimately, it still ended up with a
ban. China was an early adopter of women's football, and as far
back as 25 AD, there have been illustrations of women playing a
sport like football. The ban in China was also ahead of the rest of

the world, as the Qing Dynasty banned it in the 1640s. It lasted longer, too, several hundred years in fact; it was only lifted in 1911. During the 1920s, a teacher began a team, and more school teams started forming in the country's southeastern coastal area. When Japan invaded in 1937, football stopped in China until the 1970s.

South American countries also had female teams earlier in the twentieth century. There are records of girls playing football in a school in Chile in 1910 and other teams developed in 1919. In Argentina, there are records of a match involving women in 1913, and in Rio de Janeiro, there are records of a girls' team in 1915. In the early 1920s, several sports clubs in Brazil had girls playing, and in Argentina, there are records of two women's teams playing in front of 6,000 people. But as with everywhere else, the early promise soon came crashing down.

So, there you have it. Across the entire world, women played football, and people came to watch them. Individuals were often responsible for bringing teams together, with strong, determined women motivated simply by the desire to play a game they loved. It should have been simple. For a short time, it was. Teams appeared throughout Europe, only to disappear again as society and male football associations conspired against them. Pioneers and trailblazers brought attention to female footballers, but it was almost impossible to build anything lasting when the sport was banned to protect the men's game. But nothing is impossible, and there were many more trailblazers to come.

3

The 1940s-1950s: Rebuilding

Across Europe

Football continued in the shadows, but growth stalled as the Second World War spread across Europe. Again, despite women in Britain taking on traditional male roles during the war, once the soldiers returned, so did the gender role stereotypes. Arguably, it got worse. Women who had previously laboured in fields and assembled munitions, who had tasted freedom, were now trapped in their roles as homemakers, having to play the role of the perfect 1950s housewife.

The English FA didn't change their attitude either and upheld the ban whenever it was tested. For example, in 1947, a Kent Football Association referee who also managed Kent Ladies F.C. was suspended from refereeing because "women's football brings the game into disrepute". By managing a women's team, the FA considered he was tarnishing the men's game. Post-war attitudes hadn't changed despite the evidence that women were perfectly capable of doing physical activity — the FA's grounds for banning women on the basis of their unsuitable bodies was looking shaky.

In Scotland, the Scottish FA, who hadn't officially banned women from playing football in 1921, decided over a quarter of a century later that 1948 was the time to officially ban them from using the facilities, resources, and referees from any of their member clubs. Similarly, the German Football Association did the same but waited until 1955 before officially declaring a ban on women using affiliated pitches. Like so many football associations before them, they claimed women's bodies were too frail to compete in the sport (even more ridiculous after women had taken on so many physical roles during the war). Post-war Europe may have looked different, but its attitude towards women hadn't changed.

There was a glimmer of hope, though. Football was still quietly thriving in England, and circumstances hadn't stopped the formation of one of the most famous and successful English teams ever. Manchester Corinthians. Percy Ashley founded the team in 1949 because his daughter needed a team to play in. They played at Fog Lane Park in Didsbury and took their name from an amateur men's team who toured tirelessly to promote the men's game — something Ashley wanted to emulate with his Corinthians. The Manchester Corinthians spread the news of the resurgence of women's football as they travelled throughout England and won multiple trophies whilst doing so. They continued to win most of their matches, and Percy Ashley founded a second women's team, Nomads, in 1957 to provide local opposition. Soon, they were touring Europe.

In 1957, the team, led by Doris Ashley, toured Germany. Bert
Trautman, the German Manchester City goalkeeper, went with
them to act as their interpreter. The tour was groundbreaking,
and they played in front of 50,000-strong crowds. Their tour
ended with the 1957 unofficial European Championships
held in Germany. Although Germany officially banned women
from playing in 1955, the sport was growing quickly within
their borders. At the same time as the ban, there were
two female football associations: the German Women's
Football Association and the West German Women's Football
Association. The ban was stopping women in Germany as
little as it was in England. In 1956, Germany won their first
international when they beat the Netherlands 2-1 in front of a
crowd of 18,000 people. The German FA, the DFB, may have
banned women from playing, but apparently, nobody had got
the memo. Those who did threw it straight in the bin. Women's
football was back in Germany. And it got worse for the men at
the German FA. Not only was the ban ignored, but the number
of women playing increased rapidly. In November 1957, the
Berlin Telegraph reported that there were 28 women's football
clubs in Germany. A few months earlier, the International
Ladies Football Association was formed in Nuremberg, with
founding members Germany, Austria, the Netherlands, and
England. Like it or not, women were organising their own
game. Wasting no time, the International Ladies Football
Association arranged an unofficial Euros tournament between
the four member nations, which was held only a few months
after the association formed.

The Poststadion in Berlin hosted the 1957 Euros matches. This caused controversy as a men's match was bumped to a different stadium to allow the women's matches to go ahead. There were arguments from both sides. Some people argued women should remain banned from playing; others argued that it should be accepted and money should be made from it, since there were already thousands of active female players throughout Europe.

In any case, the tournament went ahead at the Poststadion. As the representative England team, Manchester Corinthians rounded off their tour of Germany by beating West Germany in the final to take home the 1957 European Championship trophy. The event wasn't a great showcase of German women's football on the pitch, as the team was said to have played below their best. It wasn't a great showcase off the pitch either, as the stadium clash controversy wasn't the only problem for the event. Far fewer spectators came to games, and gate receipts were much lower than the organisers had expected. Financial gaps appeared between the costs and the income, which resulted in the organisers failing to pay bills. Accusations of deliberate fraud were made, and the tournament organisers were arrested. Not what women's football needed. But the tournament had been played, and it was a step forward for the game in Europe.

Despite the Italian National Olympic Committee trying to stop the growth in the 1930s, and the Second World War doing a good job in the 1940s, teams formed again in Italy after the war. In 1946, two teams formed in Trieste, North- East Italy (Triestina and San Giusto), and football fever spread amongst women. In 1950, the

Associazione Italiana Calcio Femminile (Italian Football Women's Association) was set up in Naples. Despite continuing throughout the decade, though, no championship for women was organised. Disappointing.

It was worse in France, though, where in 1940, the pro-Nazi Vichy government upheld the football federation's ban in France. If women continued to play, there is little record of it and for the next 25 years, it was considered a sport only for men.

The Dutch Ladies Soccer Association was formed in the Netherlands in 1955, and a 14-team national league began. The national team played its first international match against Germany the same year. And then the KNVB (Dutch men's FA) banned women from their pitches. Of course, they did, just as the game was beginning to flourish. Regional leagues continued to play under the National Committee of Ladies' Soccer Association until the 1970s.

Across the rest of Europe, football had either pretty much stopped or was so far hidden in the shadows that, at this moment, there is little information on it.

Around the World

For many countries around the world, the ban in England and Europe affected the sport. In Australia, women's football was strongly discouraged, and affiliated pitches were told not to let women play. The game disappeared for decades. The story was similar in New Zealand and across the Commonwealth. It wasn't until the bans were lifted in the 1970s that football began to emerge again in these regions.

In Brazil, it was completely illegal for women to play football between 1941 and 1979. By 1940, Brazil had at least ten women's football clubs. But as the sport grew, the authorities got twitchy, and campaigners encouraged the President of the time to put a stop to it. As was the recurring theme, it was being claimed that football wasn't suitable for the female body and may pose a threat to future motherhood. The President got the Ministry of Health to investigate and banned women from playing because taking part in sport was "incompatible with the conditions of their nature". Under the new ruling, teams were forced to disband.

Although the government ban was a legal barrier, the societal ban was arguably the most significant barrier. Brazilian society believed that football was not a sport for women. Brazilian traditional values are that women should be at home as wives and mothers. During the ban, society strongly believed that football was bad for women's health and made their bodies too masculine.

Despite the illegality, women continued to play through the 1950s and 1960s. Interestingly, charity matches became the biggest driver of the sport, much like they did in England. Despite governing bodies trying to stop the games, they continued to attract media attention. Brazilian women had found a way to work around the ban. Because they helped raise money for local hospitals and schools, the communities rallied around to support the teams. So, in 1965 the government reissued the ban but took it a step further, now banning women from all sports., As a result, teams were pushed further and further from urban centres and into areas where they weren't so visible, but they continued to play. The ban remained in place until 1979 when pressure from Europe helped reverse the decision.

The first mention of women's football in Africa was in Nigeria in 1937. Matches were considered novelty games, often against unfit, middle-aged men, but they were being played. The first game documented between two women's teams was in 1944 when Onitsha Ladies took on Warri Ladies. Soon after, the ban in England filtered through, and the British colonial administration banned women from playing on association pitches. Here, as elsewhere, the women found other places to play and continued regardless.

In Canada, there is evidence that women played in Montreal in the 1950s. Local universities and colleges, including McGill University, formed teams and played against each other, but it wasn't very visible and doesn't seem to have been widespread.

The story was different in the United States, though, as their first known organised league began in 1950. Known as Craig Club, a group of 70 women from St. Louis created the first official women's football league in America. The club was named after local priest Walter Craig and was wholly inclusive: anyone could join regardless of race, religion, or background. How refreshing. Out of the 70-odd women, they formed four teams and played matches against each other. They attracted coverage from newspapers, and crowds of hundreds of people came out to watch the 15-game season. The Bobby Soccers, Coeds, Flyers, and the Bombers were teams made of tough women who, like their counterparts in other areas of the world, didn't make a big deal of their league; they simply wanted to play football. Unfortunately, the Craig Club didn't spark broader interest or kickstart a revolution. For women in St. Louis, though, it gave them somewhere to fall in love with the beautiful game.

Women's football may not have been in a strong position by the end of the 1950s, but across Europe at least, momentum was building. During the Second World War, women often took over the more physical roles of men. They realised they could contribute more to society and that their bodies could handle the physicality of sport. Although football was being played across the world, many countries still looked to the English FA for guidance, taking their cues from them. This is why so many countries across Europe and the Commonwealth banned women. But things had changed for British women since they'd virtually run the country during the war. They felt empowered and ready for change. The 1960s were coming to Britain, and anything was possible in the 1960s.

4

The 1960s: Change is Coming

The 1960s brought with it a change. Post-war Britain was coming out of the depression and was keen to create a new life filled with fun, promise, and more liberal attitudes. In a haze of drugs, free love, and musical brilliance, the nation rebelled against post-war conservatism. People began living with more freedom, excitement, fashion, and music. The Beatles summed up '60s culture and brought upbeat songs, new fashions, and worldwide celebrity. The Rolling Stones brought rock music, grit, and men your mum wouldn't have approved of. The era of the miniskirt changed fashion, broke women free from their role as 1950s housewives, and symbolised a time when they became slightly freer from the shackles of the male-dominated world. It was only the beginning, and it was going to be a slow process, but freedom for women was now on the agenda. This clear culture change helped the women's rights movement gather momentum, and women gained the confidence to question the world around them. One of those questions was, why didn't women play football?

Some women already knew the answer to that as they were playing, even though football was still banned for them, but most people didn't know they existed. The Manchester Corinthians, for example, continued to be a hugely successful team into the 1960s. Although their founder, Percy Ashley, died in 1967, the team continued to raise the profile of women's football. On the flip side, the 1960s saw the demise of Dick, Kerr Ladies. The team had been a loyal servant to the women's game, and their legacy continued, but it was time to pass the baton on. While women's football continued in the background, it was the country's excitement at the England men's team winning the World Cup in 1966 that led to the next evolution.

Women had, of course, fallen in love with the game before the men's World Cup triumph in 1966. Patricia Gregory was one of them. It was when watching her beloved Tottenham Hotspur win the 1967 FA Cup, though, that the question struck her: why don't girls play football? She was 19 years old, loved football, and it made no sense that she couldn't play. Her dad disagreed and had only reluctantly taken her to watch games because of her persistence. The more Patricia thought about it, the more annoyed she got. She did what any angry, self-respecting 19-year-old of the time would do: she wrote to the local paper. There was no social media to rant on in 1967, but there was the *Hornsey Journal*. Back then, everyone read local newspapers as their main source of information.

Patricia (known as Pat) was just a local football fan, unaware of the FA ban, who couldn't understand why men played football and women didn't. Little did she know she'd be referenced in books decades later, having become a pioneer of the game. She was never comfortable with the term "pioneer" because, in her view, she wasn't,

"We were just annoyed that we weren't allowed to do something."

The paper printed her letter and a photograph of her. Almost at once, they received replies agreeing with her. A few weeks later, her parent's living room was host to 15 young women who felt the same. They started a team. Unburdened by history, they ploughed on with their plan to play. But on talking to the council about hiring their pitch, they discovered the 1921 ban and what it meant for them: nowhere to play. Pat once again wrote to the paper. And once again, she unwittingly pushed the game forward.

A local men's team, White Star, got in touch and told Pat her team could share their facilities. Upon learning from the White Star players that Spurs used to have an amateur team called "White Ribbon", the women adopted the name for their team. With no league to join, Patricia advertised for matches in a football magazine. Only men's teams got in touch, so White Ribbon travelled up and down the country to play them. According to Patricia, the team wasn't good, but they loved playing. Most of the men they played against were mindful that they were playing women and adjusted their tackles appropriately. Although Pat remembers that "there was always one who wasn't going to be beaten by a girl".

As well as allowing Pat to get a team together and find opponents, the original newspaper article attracted the attention of Arthur Hobbs, often considered the father of women's football in

England. And this attention from Hobbs is how Pat's small action led to her being considered a pioneer.

Little did Pat Gregory and her team know, but they were not the only women looking to play football, and this was happening in pockets up and down the country. Hobbs, a carpenter from Deal in Kent, told Gregory about his newly set up tournament, the "Deal Tournament". Hobbs' vision was to showcase women's football by bringing the top teams together to compete. He believed this would provide a starting point, a ground zero to build something and give them some direction. So, he set up the tournament. When he came across Pat's White Ribbon team, he invited them to join. Of course, setting up a tournament hadn't been straightforward for Hobbs. Although Deal Town FC were keen to be hosts, the FA's ban was still in place so the Kent FA wouldn't allow the use of their ground. In protest, Deal Town's chairman and another committee member quit and wrote an angry letter to the local newspaper — it's good to remember change wouldn't have happened without the support of some men, too. Finding space for the games was difficult since, alongside the FA, many government sporting bodies were reluctant to #LetGirlsPlay.

The Kent miners, no strangers to sticking up for themselves, didn't fall into this category and allowed Hobbs to set up his tournament on the colliery playing fields. Venue sorted: Betteshanger Colliery. Game on. On a July weekend in 1967, Deal's B&Bs filled up with women keen to get on the pitch and show off their skills. This was the first time White Ribbon had met another women's team, but by the following year, word had spread, and the tournament boasted 32 teams. It was soon clear that Arthur was onto something.

As Hobbs had envisioned, they needed a focal point and some direction to set things in motion. Until then, in England at least, there had been sporadic organisation of women's matches. Now Hobbs provided a catalyst to kickstart something bigger. The 1968 Deal tournament attracted teams from further afield, including the hugely successful Manchester Corinthians.

The Women's Football Association (WFA)

Following the successful Deal tournaments, Arthur Hobbs and David Marlowe formed the Women's Football Association (WFA) in November 1969. They planned to provide organisation and structure to the game, allowing it to grow. They also looked to work with the English FA in the future, to create an official pathway for women's football in England.

A staggering 44 teams attended the first meeting of the WFA in London. Patricia Dunn was elected as the first chair but wasn't in post long before she was asked to resign because the FA preferred to have a man in charge. Pat Gwynne became chair, and Patricia Dunn became vice-chair. Six months after their first meeting, the 44 teams, arranged into seven regional leagues, had their first Annual General Meeting (AGM). The association's first secretary was Arthur Hobbs, but poor health forced him to retire in 1972. Patricia Gregory, the girl who began her football career writing an advert in her local paper, became the secretary of the WFA for the next decade.

Florence (known as Flo) Bilton also played a major role in the WFA. She helped form it in 1969 and was part of the administrative staff between 1969 and 1993 (when the FA took over running it).

Profile: Flo Bilton

Flo, born in 1921, played many roles for young female footballers in England. In 1963, she started a team at the Reckitt & Colman factory, in Hull, where she worked. The team played their first game against neighbouring factory, Smith & Nephew, and won 2-1. Flo was their veteran goalkeeper.

She took on numerous roles at the WFA, helping in any way to improve the standards and opportunities for the players. She was instrumental in organising football in Hull, helping local players like Carol Thomas to progress into the England team. This is how Carol described her:

"Hull was the birthplace of the indomitable Flo Bilton, a force of nature. Even though women were banned from playing on FA-affiliated pitches, Flo had already set up the Hull Women's Football League with about 8/9 teams. She also became a member of the Women's Football Association committee. Becoming the England team chaperone, amongst other roles. She was very influential in my life, keeping me grounded and helping me with travel and the rest. I owe her so much. "

Flo wasn't afraid to get stuck in and take on extra roles either, including washing players' kits by hand. After the official England

women's team formed in 1972, Flo got hold of a men's England
cap from her neighbour in Hull and used it as a template to make
copies for the England women, so they didn't miss out on this
international rite of passage — although they only got one or two
because making a cap for every player for every game was a bit
much, even for Flo. She chaperoned the team, stitched badges onto
kits, and put the WFA newsletter together. In short, Flo Bilton
played a massive role for the WFA and early England teams.

Harry Batt and His Unofficial England Team

Whilst Patricia Gregory, Arthur Hobbs, and the WFA were
going through official channels to set up a new era for football
alongside the FA in England, Harry Batt was forging a different
path. Batt didn't want to wait until the FA were ready for an
England women's team and had his sights set on creating his own
(unofficial) England side, independent of the WFA and FA. Batt's
involvement with women's football was both glorious and tragic.

In 1967, along with his wife June, he formed the Chiltern Valley
Ladies team in Luton. Bus driver by day and a football visionary by
night, Batt wanted to showcase the women's game despite the ban.
He scouted players from local boy's teams to find the girls who had
disguised themselves as boys so they could play. Harry hand-picked
them to recruit into his new team and they played as the Chiltern
Valley Ladies. It wasn't long before Batt took them to tournaments
as an unofficial England team. The Chiltern Valley Ladies found
international fame as The British Independents when they took

to the world stage a few years later (more on their story in the next chapter).

The Rest of the British Isles

The history of Scottish women's football during the intervening decades remains largely unknown, but the 1960s marked the start of the modern football era in Scotland. Again, factories and workplaces provided the backdrop for new teams. The first of these formed in 1961 as Stewarton Thistle from Kilmarnock, Ayr. Now named Kilmarnock FC Women, it is the oldest women's team in Scotland. This was how young Elsie Cook — who later became Scotland manager and secretary of the Scottish Women's Football Association — got into football. Aged 14, she helped her mum form the Stewarton Thistle team. She played in the team's defence with her mum and two aunties. Elsie was instrumental in moving the game forward for women and girls after she was inspired by the talented 17-year-old Susan Ferries. In their first game, a charity match, Susan scored all seven of the team's goals in her cheap second-hand boots, and it was then Elsie knew she had to fight for the rights of women to play,

"After that day, that was me on a mission to prove to men and to women that lassies could play football and it was because of Susan Ferries," Elsie told *The Scotsman* in 2021.

She told the *Daily Record* in 2023 that,

"I made this my life's mission to expand the game of football for girls and women of all ages from Under-9s to adults. I became a football Suffragette from 1961 until 1993."

And she did. Elsie later coached Stewarton Thistle to the first Women's FA Cup final in 1971, became secretary of the Scottish Women's Football Association, got the ban overturned in Scotland, and briefly managed the Scottish national team.

In 1965, an enthusiastic and game-changing young player named Rose Reilly joined Elsie's Stewarton Thistle. Rose was a local girl and an exceptionally talented striker. At 10 years old, she made her debut for Stewarton Thistle Ladies, and throughout her career, Elsie was there to support and encourage her (more on Rose later). Other teams followed Stewarton, including Fife Dynamites, Cambuslang Hooverettes, Holyrood Bumbees, Tayside Toppers, and Westthorn United. Stewarton and Westthorn became the best two teams in the country and regularly battled it out for honours.

More teams formed in Scotland as the decade went on, and in 1967, a TV star of the time — Hughie Green — had an idea for a women's football tournament. He got a Scottish female sponsor involved, and the event developed into regional tournaments hosted by Butlins. The tournament, held throughout the country, finished with a grand final in London. Westthorn United beat Stewarton Thistle to win the Scottish region and played in the first Butlins' Cup final against Fodens of Cheshire. The final finished 0-0 after extra time, and a few days later, Fodens won the replay played in Glasgow.

In 1968, Scotland's first organised league began. Despite continued opposition from the governing body, women's football began to build its own organisational structure.

Throughout the 1960s, there seems to have been little football activity in Wales or Northern Ireland. In the Republic of Ireland, organised football appeared in 1965 when Benfica, one of the oldest Irish clubs, formed in Waterford, Munster. Games between university teams began in 1967, and by the end of the decade, football had started to become organised.

Across Europe

Football developed and expanded throughout Europe. Despite continued bans, more teams formed in Germany, France, and Italy. Regional leagues were being formed too, but there was growing frustration at the lack of international tournaments.

In France, teams began to form in the mid-sixties despite the ban. Things really kicked off (pun intended) in 1968 when a journalist, Pierre Geoffroy, called for interested women to contact him about playing a match at a local annual fair. Fifteen women replied, and Geoffroy unwittingly became the godfather of modern women's football in France. Geoffroy's project to build a team for an exhibition game at the local fair turned into the formation of club side Reims. Reims became pioneers and led the way in promoting women's football in France. Other teams formed on the back of Reims visibility, including in Lyon and Paris. In 1969, an unofficial French national team began to play friendlies against England and Italy.

Football also began in Sweden when Öxabäcks IF started a team in 1966. By the end of the decade, other teams had formed, and they organised an eight-team competition. A competition

for girls, the St. Eriks Cup, began in 1969, and 35 teams were
involved. The stage was set for future success in Sweden. In
Denmark too, women's football became established in the 1960s
when the Danish Women's Football Union began organising the
game. In 1969, East and West leagues formed, and the winners
of each league competed in a final. Femina BK won the first
title and represented Denmark in the four-nations European
Championship in Italy in 1969.

Football began to bubble up in several areas across Europe, but
it was Italy who pushed it forward. By the end of the 1960s,
the Italians had waited long enough for the governing bodies of
men's football to endorse women, and they began organising their
own tournaments. They became the beacon of hope for female
footballers across the world. In 1968, the Federazione Italiana
Calcio Femminile (FICF), the Italian Women's Federation,
formed and quickly set up their first organised league, marking
the start of the Serie A Femminile. The league began with two
groups of five teams, with a final held in Pisa. A.C.F. Genova
(Genoa) beat Rome to win the first Serie A title. The same year,
the Italian national team played their first international match
against Czechoslovakia. Having already set up the Serie A league
and played their first international, the Italians were keen to
expand their football horizons and began organising international
tournaments.

In 1969, the recently formed FICF organised what is now
considered a precursor to the UEFA Women's Euros, a European
competition for four national teams. Some Italian businessmen

saw the opportunity that women's football provided after seeing the crowds that came to watch. The Coppa Europa per Nazioni was born. The drinks company Martini & Rossi sponsored the tournament and paid for accommodation and travel, allowing Italy, England, France, and Denmark to take part.

England's newly formed WFA declined an invitation to send a team, as they hadn't yet formed an official national team and considered it "too short notice". So, Harry Batt, who was already known to the Italian organisers, was asked if he'd put together a team instead. Never one to shirk a challenge, he did, and they flew to Europe, courtesy of Martini & Rossi. The players came from Batt's Chiltern Ladies team, Southampton, Luton, and Kays Ladies.

With just four teams, the tournament consisted of a semi-final and a final. Despite Sue Lopez netting a hat-trick for the unofficial Lionesses, Denmark, represented by Femina BK, beat England 4-3 in their semi-final. Italy beat Pierre Geoffroy's France 1-0. England beat France in the third-place play-off in front of a crowd of 10,000 people and hosts Italy beat Denmark 3-1 in the final to take the 1969 Euros title. Sue Lopez of England finished the tournament as the top scorer with four goals.

Unlike the tournament in Germany in 1957, the 1969 tournament was a huge success, on and off the pitch. The commercial success prompted the Italian Federation to continue organising major football tournaments. UEFA wasn't impressed, and FIFA "investigated" the 1969 event. But neither was a match for the Italian's love of football, and the show went on.

Across the rest of the world, there was little visible evidence of girls and women playing, but there were reports of girls' teams beginning to form in Canada, Nigeria, and South Africa.

The sixties had started a revolution, not just in fashion and music, but in football. Patricia Gregory and Arthur Hobbs had formed the enduring Women's Football Association in England, Elsie Cook put women footballers at the top of her agenda in Scotland, and Pierre Geoffroy put the pieces together in France. As democracy slowed any advancement between the FA and the WFA in England, Harry Batt formed his own England team, which played throughout Europe. He was helped by a group of Italians who were about to shake up the world of football.

5

The 1970s, Part 1: Lifting the Ban

The English FA had come under increasing pressure to lift the ban. For just shy of 50 years, women were banned in England, but the growth in the sport and the determination of those involved continued. Ultimately, this persistence helped twist the FA's arm. Late in December 1969, part of the FA's committee agreed they should lift the ban. On the 19th of January 1970, the English FA officially voted to reverse the ban on women playing football on their pitches. Although lifting the ban didn't change anything at this point and the FA didn't really plan to support women playing, it started a new era of football in England and throughout Europe.

First WFA Cup in England

The WFA didn't waste time once the ban was lifted, and the first English national knockout cup started in the 1970/71 season. The WFA Cup was open to clubs from all over Great Britain. In its early days, the cup was known as The Women's Football Association

Mitre Challenge Trophy, named after its sponsor, Mitre. Now, it is simply known as The Women's FA Cup.

In its first year, the WFA Cup attracted 71 teams who wanted to compete, including teams from Scotland and Wales. Organised into eight groups based on geography, the teams battled it out to be group winners before moving to the quarter-final stage.

England's Southampton Women and Scotland's Stewarton Thistle contested the first final at Crystal Palace National Sports Centre. The WFA had to rely on smaller venues hosting the final because although the FA had lifted the ban, the English Football League still didn't want to allow women to play their FA Cup final on their pitches. This didn't change until over a decade later when Queen's Park Rangers' Loftus Road was the first league ground to host the final in 1982.

The first Mitre Challenge Trophy was won by Southampton, in the first of their eight WFA Cup wins. Southampton Women FC was a force to be reckoned with during this period. Founded in 1970, the team was hugely successful throughout the decade. They began after England's men won the 1966 World Cup. Women working at Cunard's shipping company expressed an interest in playing, and the company helped develop the team. The secretary of the social club at Cunard, Hank Coombes, encouraged other companies to start teams, and they began playing friendlies against each other. The local newspaper, the *Southern Evening Echo*, was supportive, and matches were played for charity to help increase support from the public. More company teams formed, and they set up a Southampton league, which played its first games in September 1966. As the first season progressed, a committee selected the top players from the league to form the Southampton team. They played their first match against a team from Portsmouth in the pouring rain and won 5-0. Southampton Women's FC was born. They won seven more WFA Cup finals over the next decade and picked up their last Women's FA Cup trophy in 1981.

Europe Begins to Lift the Ban

Following the lead of the English FA, on the 23rd of March 1970, the French Football Federation lifted its ban on women playing football. Later that year, a national team formed and toured Canada and the USA. On 17th April 1971, France played against the Netherlands in what, at the time, was just another friendly. But in the early 2000s, when FIFA needed to set up a world ranking system for women, they (somewhat randomly) designated this 1971 game as the first official women's international. Even more oddly, the game acted as a qualifying match for the 1971 World Cup in Mexico, a tournament that FIFA strongly opposed. The match was played in the Northern French town of Hazebrouck in March 1971; this was a big step forward, especially if you consider that six years earlier, *France Football* magazine had declared, "all organised attempts can only be doomed to failure... in our opinion, football is only for men".

Pierre Geoffroy clearly disagreed. Having gone from gathering a team for a local fair to founding the successful club side Reims, he managed the French national team (which consisted of many Reims players). His team played this historic fixture, which attracted 1500 spectators. It received little media attention, but France came out as 4-0 winners, thanks mainly to a hat-trick from Jocelyne Ratignier. Although the players didn't know this before the game, winning meant they had qualified for the 1971 (unofficial) World Cup in Mexico.

Meanwhile, as other football associations lifted their bans and UEFA pondered their next move, the group of Italian businessmen continued to take advantage of the growing interest in women's football and organised more international tournaments.

The 1970 Coppa del Mondo

Having organised a successful 1969 Euros, the Italian women's football federation, along with sponsors Martini & Rossi (the alcoholic drinks maker — yes, that Martini, shaken, not stirred), organised the Coppa del Mondo (World Cup) in 1970.

Football was still banned or, at least, inhibited in many countries, so the tournament — also known as the Martini and Rossi Cup — remained unofficial and at odds with UEFA and FIFA. The Women's Football Association (WFA) in England was trying to negotiate with the FA to get an official Lionesses team formed when the tournament was being organised. They didn't want to take part in unsanctioned tournaments that may undermine their efforts. So, Harry Batt once again stepped in and formed a representative England team. He essentially brought his Chiltern Valley Ladies team over to Italy for the World Cup. Since they were unofficial and unable to be called England, they went under the banner of "The British Independents". Everyone knew them as England.

Seven teams competed in the tournament, transported and accommodated at the expense of chief sponsors Martini & Rossi. Eight teams were due to take part, but Czechoslovakia were forced to withdraw because they couldn't get visas. Denmark, Italy, Mexico, England, West Germany, Austria, and Switzerland competed in the first (unofficial) World Cup.

England beat West Germany 5-1 on the opening day: I say this for historical completeness, you understand, not because England has spent many years being beaten by German sides since then. Mexico, who turned out to be a surprise package, beat Austria 9-0. Harry Batt's England lost to Denmark in the semi-finals, and Italy saw off Mexico.

Represented by the team Boldklubben Femina (established in 1959), Denmark beat the hosts in front of 40,000 spectators in the Turin-hosted final. Mexico beat England in the third- place play-off.

The tournament was another success for the organisers, so they spread their wings further and took their product to Mexico.

Copa '71: Mexico World Cup

Women's football was gathering pace across the world by now and in 1971, the Federation of Independent European Female Football

(FIEFF), with help from sponsors Martini & Rossi, organised the second (unofficial) women's World Cup in Mexico.

Known as the Campeonato de Fútbol Femenil (Women's Soccer Championship), the Mexican World Cup nearly didn't happen as FIFA tried to ban it. However, with the Italians, the drink manufacturers, and the Mexican football federation seeing the rise in interest in women's football (and the potential to make money), they were undeterred and put on a magnificent event. Now more commonly known as Copa '71, thanks to the film of the same name, the Mexico World Cup should have been a game-changer for women's football.

The Mexican federation promoted the six-team tournament in the same way they had promoted the men's World Cup in 1970. They were commercially astute, making merchandise featuring the mascot, Xochitl, a young girl dressed in the Mexico kit, holding a football. They aimed to appeal to a female and family-friendly audience, too, by decorating the goalposts in pink and giving tournament staff pink uniforms. They also weren't against using the feminine angle to promote the tournament to men: the mascot, for all her positive strong feminine icon vibe, also had pigtails and an hourglass figure. This time they promoted the heck out of their women's World Cup. The promotion worked, and Mexicans came out in their tens of thousands to watch the matches at the iconic Azteca stadium (now immortalised in the film Copa '71, which really showcases the event).

The Women's Football Association (WFA) in England was still trying to make progress with the FA at this point. They hadn't formed an official England women's team and didn't want to rock the boat with the FA while trying to make progress within the administration. Again, the WFA turned down the opportunity to send a team, and again, Harry Batt was only too happy to raise a team to represent England.

But the tournament was played across three weeks in the summer. Many of Batt's previous "British Independents" worked and couldn't leave their paid jobs for a long jolly to South America. Harry had to find replacements. He scouted local teams for players, but his squad ended up being mainly built from local teenagers, including 14-year-old Gill Sayell from Milton Keynes, 15-year-old Chris Lockwood, and 13-year-old Leah Caleb because they would be off school for the summer. Imagine you're a teenager about to start your summer holidays when you're plucked from your local team and given the chance to play for England in Mexico. Some of them didn't even have a passport.

Since Batt's team was in direct opposition to the WFA's plans to form an official team, it was considered unofficial and not recognised by the FA. As they weren't allowed to compete as "England", Harry's team remained known as "The British Independents". Away from the politics, the team flew to Mexico thanks to the continued generosity of Martini & Rossi, who paid their travel and accommodation expenses. The Mexicans hadn't received the memo about the English FA's politics, so they embraced the players as "Inglaterra". Batt's England, chaperoned by referee Pat Dunn, was received warmly in Mexico and treated like superstars by the press and the fans. Camera shutters clicked as they descended the plane steps, something the players had never experienced before. The young footballers played amongst the shadows in their home country, but Mexico fully embraced them; hundreds of fans even arrived at the team's early morning training sessions, hoping for autographs.

Argentina, Italy, Denmark, Mexico, and France also competed in the event. Although the World Cup itself was unofficial and unrecognised by most football associations, the Italian Football Federation classed all of Italy's 1971 games as full internationals.

The teams drew big crowds as Mexico embraced women's football. The British Independents' game against Mexico was played in front of 80,000 people at the massive Azteca stadium in Mexico City. But if the prospect of pigtails and perfect figures of femininity on the pitch had seduced the men in the crowd, they were soon disappointed. In England's first game against Argentina, the tackles were so brutal that captain Carol Wilson and their right back, Yvonne Farr, both broke their legs. During the Mexico vs Italy semi-final, and after a few dubious refereeing decisions — including two goals disallowed for Italy — some of the Italian players couldn't keep their anger inside, and fists flew. The game was abandoned 10 minutes early.

Mexico and Denmark contested the final, played out in front of 110,000 fans at the Azteca Stadium. It was an incredible occasion with a carnival atmosphere and no expense spared on the razzmatazz of a big sporting event: once in a lifetime for these women. The Danish team ran rings around Mexico, and a hat-trick by 15-year-old Susanne Augustesen meant the tournament ended with Denmark winning their second major trophy in a row. The Danish team arrived home and were greeted by the press and fans. They naturally thought this was it; women's football was on the map. But soon after, everything went quiet, and nobody talked about their win again. Women's football remained in the shadows. The Danish Football Association didn't recognise the win at all.

Throughout the tournament, the British Independents had police escorts to travel to matches because wherever they went, fans wanted to shake their hands or get them to sign autographs. This adoration was confined to Mexico. When they touched down back at home in England, their reception wasn't remotely warm. Rather than a heroes' welcome for the returning players, who were playing in front of tens of thousands of people days before, the women were welcomed home with an FA ban. The players were banned for several months, and many never recovered from this treatment, having been made to feel like they'd done something wrong. Harry Batt's treatment was worse, and he was banned from coaching for life. His teams disbanded, and he was left devastated.

Although Harry and many of the women in his team never recovered from this humiliation and were never recognised as an England team, they will always be an important part of the story in England. I love the "Independents" story because it is about getting on the pitch and playing the game, not about politics. Not everyone agreed, and Batt's way was considered the "wrong" way. It showed the passion of the players and the spectators who fell in love with "Inglaterra" around the world, though. Those tournaments, with their massive crowds, set in motion the plans for football's "official" governing body-recognised tournaments.

6

The 1970s, Part 2: UEFA Rethink

Although the treatment of the teams returning from Mexico was devastating, they had sparked debate within UEFA. The federation knew they couldn't ignore the popularity of the unofficial tournaments any longer. The vast crowds in Mexico and the growing enthusiasm for women's football made them realise things had to change.

A report from UEFA in November 1970 showed how the game was growing behind their backs. They weren't exactly interested in supporting women playing and didn't feel a sudden urge to offer equality. They were, however, concerned that "wily business managers" would continue to organise major international tournaments and that they would lose control of the game.

In 1971, UEFA couldn't ignore the growth across Europe any longer. They sent a letter to the individual associations looking for information on how much football was being played by women in the countries under their control. Out of 22 European nations where women played, only eight were under the control of the national governing body (and therefore within UEFA's control). They realised they had to bring the sport under their umbrella quickly so they could control the game and the resulting competitions. They asked their 32 member countries to vote on whether they should overturn the ban and allow individual countries to decide how they governed the game in the future. Thirty-one of the 32 member countries agreed to drop the ban and bring the sport in Europe under UEFA's control. The only country that voted to continue the ban was Scotland.

The first UEFA women's football committee was set up and began standardising the game. Sweden's Kerstin Rosén became the first female member of any UEFA committee. The survey had shown that some associations ran national women's championships, and some ran regional leagues. There was some support for introducing a UEFA-managed international competition, but opinion was divided. They decided to focus on regulating women's football under UEFA control before organising a major competition.

Growth of the game slowed, and UEFA cited the same obstacles to major competition when they met in 1974, presumably trying to stall the development of the game. They didn't have another meeting before the committee dissolved four years later in 1978, having done absolutely nothing in the intervening years.

UEFA may have set up a committee for women's football, but during the next seven years, it failed to organise a single international women's competition. They had successfully stopped the "wily" businessmen from organising such events and had stalled the progress of women's football for the best part of another decade.

Back in Scotland, their country's vote to keep the ban in place was a blow. Elsie Cook and others responded by setting up the Scottish Women's Football Association (SWFA) in 1972. Elsie became the SWFA's first secretary and spent the next few years campaigning to reverse the ban.

The SWFA wasted no time in organising a match against England. In November 1972, Ravenscraig Stadium in Greenock, Scotland, hosted the first official international match played in Great Britain (since England were now officially recognised by the FA). The venue was used for athletics, but because of the Scottish Football Association (SFA) ban, they could not use an SFA-affiliated pitch. Despite the obstacles, Patricia Gregory from the WFA in England and Elsie Cook, the SWFA secretary in Scotland, organised the logistics, including a pitch, officials, and travel for the teams.

Through trials, the WFA selected a new team to represent England for their first international. Manager Eric Worthington led the England squad of 17 women: Sue Buckett, Morag Kirkland, Sandra Graham, Janet Bagguley, Sheila Parker, Paddy McGroarty, Lynda Hale, Sylvia Gore, Pat Davies, Jeannie Allott, Jean Wilson, Susan Whyatt, Wendy Owen, Julia Manning, Eileen Foreman, Pat Firth, and Maggie Miks.

The Scottish squad, led by manager Robert Stewart, included 16 women: Janie Houghton, Jean Hunter, June Hunter, Linda Kidd, Marian Mount, Sandra Walker, Rose Reilly, Edna Neillis, Mary Anderson, Margaret McAuley, Mary Carr, Liz Creamer, Mary Davenport, Linda Cooper, Diane McLaren, and Irene Morrison.

In a game played in snowy conditions, Scotland went 2-0 up through goals from Mary Carr and Rose Reilly. England came back and eventually won 3-2 with goals from Sylvia Gore, Lynda Hale, and Jeannie Allott. The real victory though, was for women's football. The game took place almost exactly one hundred years after the first official men's international between the two teams (although there was the unofficial Scotland vs England match in 1881). It's recorded as the second official women's international recognised by FIFA after France v Netherlands in 1971 was retrospectively appointed the first.

Fifty years later, in 2022, that very first official England team was finally fully recognised: previously, they'd never received caps. This was fixed when the first official Lionesses were presented with their caps and given legacy FA numbers. Fifty years on from that first match, the team got to walk around Wembley's pitch to receive applause from the 76,000 people there to watch the European Champions, England, play against the USA — the Lionesses first game back at Wembley since the Euros victory. It was a special moment for women's football in England.

Scotland's domestic league was developing too. In 1972, the Scottish Women's Football Association began with six teams:

Profile: Sheila Parker, England captain

Sheila Parker was England's captain for the first official England v Scotland game by manager Eric Worthington. Sheila began her football career with Dick, Kerr Ladies. The Lancashire defender played under four different England managers in the four years she was captain. She continued her international career until May 1983, when she retired, having played 33 games for her country. She won the WFA Cup with Fodens in 1974, before moving to Preston North End in 1975. During that season, she scored 51 goals in 14 games, which helped Preston win the Division One league title. She won more league and cup titles with Preston before moving to St. Helens.

Sheila played and managed her home team, Chorley Ladies FC, before having one last crack at the big time. In 1989, she moved to Wigan Ladies FC, won two league titles, and promotion to Division One in 1990 with them. Sheila retired from playing football at the age of 46 after 34 years as a player. Then, she qualified as a referee. In 2013, she was inducted into the National Football Museum Hall of Fame, having won six Division One titles and five League Cups.

Aberdeen, Edinburgh Dynamos, Westthorn United, Motherwell AEI, Dundee Strikers, and Stewarton Thistle. Their first winner was Westthorn United, who also competed in the Women's FA Cup final in 1973. Under continued pressure from UEFA, the Scottish Women's FA (SWFA), and Elsie Cook, the male Scottish Football Association (SFA) had no choice but to remove their ban. After UEFA threatened to give them financial penalties in 1974, the SFA reluctantly caved in.

To celebrate the lifting of the ban, the Scottish international team played on an SFA-affiliated pitch for the first time. In September 1974.

Profile: Margaret McAulay, Scotland captain

Margaret McAulay was Scotland's first official captain in 1972. She was a brilliant midfielder who loved to score. She played over 20 times for her country and captained her club, Westthorn United. She won the Scottish Women's Cup and the Scottish Women's League Cup and reached the Women's FA Cup final.

She described to the current Glasgow Rangers women's squad in 2023 how she was surprised to be named as captain for the first official international between Scotland and England, but was "overjoyed" because it was such a great honour to captain Scotland.

At Celtic Park, the team took on a Scottish Select team featuring the best of the rest of Scotland's talent. Despite the Scottish FA officially endorsing women playing football in Scotland, they weren't yet ready to accept it.

Two big names in women's football, Scottish players Rose Reilly and Edna Neillis, moved to Europe during the 1970s to become professional footballers, something unavailable to them in Britain. They both moved to Reims in France and then on to A.C.F. Milan in Italy. Whilst there, they learned how much better supported female footballers were in these countries and called for the Scottish FA to improve their support of women's football in Scotland. Elsie Cook, SWFA secretary and briefly their national team coach, agreed with Rose and Edna and spoke out too. Soon after, the SFA banned both women from ever playing for Scotland again and disciplined Elsie Cook. The women led a protest march in Glasgow against the suspensions, but the SFA didn't budge, and Rose and Edna never played for Scotland again.

Scotland's loss became Italy's gain, thanks to Rose Reilly's fascinating and unusual place in footballing history. Rose was seven when she joined her local boys' team, Stewarton United. She was able to join the club if she kept her hair short and went by the name of Ross. She was a talented striker and attracted the attention of Celtic scouts. However, their interest cooled when they realised "Ross" was actually "Rose".

In the mid-1960s, she made her debut for Stewarton United Ladies and was part of the team when they lifted the Scottish Cup in 1971. The same year, they reached the final of the first WFA Cup. In 1972, she moved to Westthorn United, where she won the treble of the Scottish League, Scottish Cup, and the League Championship. As much as she loved her home country, though, Scotland couldn't provide what Rose craved. She didn't want to do anything else with her life. She wanted to make football her career. The 17-year-old trailblazer packed her bags and took her dreams to Europe. After a brief spell with French team Reims, she moved to AC Milan and essentially became Italian. Having arrived not knowing a word of the language, she threw herself into Italian culture to connect with her new teammates. It was a different world: from pretending to be a boy to playing professionally at the San Siro stadium — she was realising her dreams.

Between 1972 and 1973, Rose made ten appearances for Scotland before being banned for life from playing for them. The concept of nationality was clearly more fluid back then, and although Rose

had no connection to Italy before joining Milan, she began playing
for the Italian national side. It was an astute move by Italy. In
1984, she won the Mundialito, considered a forerunner of the
World Cup, with Italy and was voted best Italian player of the
tournament. By the time she had retired at age 40, she had won
eight Serie A league titles with various Italian clubs, four Italian
Cups, and a French league title. She won the Serie A Golden Boot
in 1978 and 1981 and won a World Cup. In 2007, she was inducted
into the Scottish Football Hall of Fame.

Football picked up across the rest of the British Isles, too. Wales
and the Republic of Ireland played their first international in
1973, shortly after the Women's Football Association of Ireland
was formed. In November 1976, the Northern Ireland Women's
Football Association (NIWFA) formed after their first meeting
in a Post Office Youth Club in Belfast. In 1977, the NIWFA
formed a three-division league of 18 teams and played their first
international against the Republic of Ireland in the same year.
British football was gathering pace again, and a revolution was
starting across the world.

7

The 1970s, Part 3: Global Development

Football fever spread. From massive unofficial World Cups to small local tournaments, women wanted to play football wherever they were in the world. The lifting of the ban in England opened the gates for legitimate organisation across much of the globe. Women's love for football led to the organisation of domestic competitions and international trophy events in virtually every corner of the world. This was a breakthrough decade and although much of society still felt it inappropriate for women to play a contact sport, many football associations had to accept that women were going to play football.

In the 1960s, Pierre Geoffroy became the driving force behind reinvigorating women's football in France. "Mister Geoffroy", as he was known, helped form the club Stade de Reims Féminines in 1968, and the team became the figurehead for women's football across Europe. In 1974, the French women's championship — Division 1 Féminine — restarted under the French Football Federation, and Reims dominated it. They built their skill and reputation by playing warm-up matches before men's games and by touring the world. They were already widely known when they toured Ireland in 1973, and it was on the tours that they spotted local talent.

In Ireland in 1973, that talent was 17-year-old Anne O'Brien from Dublin. Geoffroy asked her to join Reims, and she played a few games with them before signing. Because she was so young, she had to wait until she was 18 before she could decide to move to France to play. Although women weren't allowed to play professional football in France, Reims worked around this to give players semi-professional football. They offered players contracts to work at local factories and other businesses and also arranged and paid for accommodation.

Anne O'Brien was offered a part-time job with a factory but was allowed plenty of time off for training and matches. Anne O'Brien wasn't the first overseas player to play professionally in Europe under similar arrangements. Sue Lopez of England had joined the Italian club Torino in 1969, for example, but it was Anne's move that generated the most publicity and interest in Britain and Ireland. Reims continued to spot overseas talent and later that year signed Scottish players Rose Reilly and Edna Neillis on similar contracts, allowing them to play what was considered professional football: something they couldn't do at home.

In 1975 the French Football Federation officially reinstated women's football and began funding their first division. Between 1975 and 1982, Reims won five titles, and the team made up most of the France national team who played in front of 60,000 people in the Azteca Stadium in Mexico in 1971.

France had Reims to bring across foreign players, but it was Italy who attracted the most foreign players. By 1972, forty-six clubs were competing in four regions of Italy, and the sport continued to grow under its current women's governing body. The Italian FA had voted for women's football to be reinstated by FIFA but was happy for it to continue running as it was before, under the Italian Federation of Female Football (FFIGC). Through the 1970s, Italy was among the first nations to offer what was considered professional football. They imported players from all over Europe to star in their recently founded Serie A league. The clubs made individual agreements with players, finding them flexible jobs to train around and sometimes paying for accommodation (like at Reims). Rose Reilly was the biggest star to move to Italy.

In the 1970s, Germany began to build the foundations of its future footballing empire. Founded in 1969, TuS Wörrstadt were pioneers of league football in Germany. In 1970, Bayern Munich's women's team formed for the first time, and other teams soon followed. When the German FA failed to set up a women's championship, TuS Wörrstadt organised one themselves (and won it). In 1974, the first women's league championship was established, this time by the German FA. Only a few years after the ban was lifted, the Deutscher Fußball-Bund (the German FA) appointed Hannelore Ratzeburg as the first woman on the committee in charge of representing women's football in Germany.

In Spain, football for women remained officially outlawed through the first half of the 1970s, but clubs appeared anyway. On Christmas Day 1970, FC Barcelona women's team played their first match at the mighty Nou Camp stadium. Players weren't allowed to wear a Barcelona kit, so they played as Selecció Ciutat de Barcelona. However, they were coached by Barcelona's club legend goalkeeper, Antonio Ramallets. They played as part of a charity festival for local children's hospitals, which also featured Barcelona's men's first team against CSKA Sofia: 60,000 fans came to watch the double-header.

Barcelona's women's team began when 18-year-old Immaculada Cabecerán (affectionately known as Imma) told Barca's president, Agusti Montal, that girls wanted to play football. Despite the ban, he told her if she could find enough players for a team, the club would support it. As is now tradition, Imma placed an advert in a magazine. She soon found enough players to form the first Barcelona women's team. Antonio Ramallets coached them for the next two years. Although this was the start of FC Barcelona Women, the club didn't officially recognise them until 2002. Meanwhile, an unofficial Spanish national team formed, and in February 1971, they played their debut against Portugal. Their first game abroad came a few months later against Italy, and Spain's first domestic league began in the 1971/72 season. Not bad for a country where the sport was still banned.

Denmark were runners-up in the 1969 Euros in Italy but began the 1970s by winning both the Coppa Del Mondo in Italy in 1970 and the 1971 Mexico World Cup (Copa '71). With young star

Susanne Augustesen's hat-trick winning Denmark's second World Cup in a row, the team should have been megastars; we should all know Susanne's name. After all, Pele's Brazil had won their third men's World Cup trophy only a year ago in the same stadium. And we've all heard of Pele. This was the world these women played in: there was no recognition, despite heroic feats that at least matched the men's teams of the time. In 1973, the first Danish FA-organised leagues began and a year later, Denmark played their first official international against Sweden. They topped off the decade by winning the 1979 Euros in Italy. But just like in many other countries, their football associations failed them by not giving them sufficient support and finances to help them grow, which halted any progress.

Sweden and Norway were slightly behind Denmark in their evolution but soon became major players on the international scene thanks to the support of their football associations. No organised football in Sweden was recorded before 1966, but it quickly grew over the next few years. In 1971, 17 of Sweden's 24 district associations organised competitions, and in 1972, the first national championship took place. A year later, Sweden played their first international against Finland, and in 1978, the Swedish FA took control of women's football. Unlike other nations throughout Europe, Sweden had a strong ethos around equality. So, rather than stifling the growth of women's football, Sweden put resources into building a strong team, which set them up for an excellent future.

Women's football in Finland also grew in popularity. In 1971, a summer national tournament of six teams took place, and after UEFA's vote, the Finnish FA accepted women's football and brought it under their control. Within a year, a domestic competition was established, and a whopping 51 teams took part in the first year. The first final was held at the Helsinki Olympic Stadium. In year two of Finland's football venture, the number of female players more than doubled. However, as the game got more serious, the novelty wore off, and the number of players stalled. The sport didn't spread as hoped, partly due to a lack of funds and partly due to fewer girls' teams being set up. Over the next decade, the number of registered players hardly rose at all.

Norway's development began later in the decade when, in 1975, a women's football committee was first set up. A year later, the Norwegian Football Federation officially recognised women players, and in 1978, the Norway national team played their first international match against Sweden. Their first regional league began at the end of the 1970s, but their major wins will come later in our story.

The Nordic teams experienced international competitive tournaments from 1974 when the first women's Nordic Championship was held in Finland between Denmark, Sweden, and the host nation. Denmark, with their international experience, won the inaugural tournament. Over the course of the three matches, an average of around 900 people came to watch. For the next few years, Denmark dominated the competition, but in 1977, with Norway now taking part too, Sweden won their first title. The Nordic Championships stopped in 1982.

Whilst football continued throughout Europe, UEFA was still dragging its heels about organising a major competition, still doing its best to stifle the life out of the game with bureaucracy and inaction. True to form, Italy wasn't standing for it, and in 1979, the Italian women's federation hosted another international competition. Twelve teams took part in the 1979 European Championships. Italy, Norway, Northern Ireland, England, Finland, Switzerland, Denmark, France, Scotland, Sweden, Netherlands, and Wales competed in an event much larger than previous competitions. Denmark took the title in a final played in front of 15,000 spectators in Naples. The third-place playoff between Sweden and England went to penalties, which Sweden won. In a meeting in February 1980, UEFA described the 1979 tournament as a "cause for concern" and decided they had to launch their own competition. About time.

Football was developing throughout the rest of the world, too. The Asian Ladies Football Confederation (ALFC), founded in 1968, started the Asian Women's Championship (later the Women's Asian Cup) in 1975. Throughout the early part of its history, the competition was held every two or three years, but it's now held every four years and acts as a FIFA World Cup qualification competition. It was instrumental in developing football in Asia.

In Australia in 1974, the men's team qualified for a World Cup for the first time, bringing more attention to football in their country. Women benefited from this new interest in association rules football (as opposed to Aussie rules), and leagues began in most states. In August 1974, Dr. Oscar Mate and Pat O'Connor organised the first national championship. The first National Women's Soccer Championships were held over a week in Sydney. Five teams took part: New South Wales, Macquarie and Districts (Northern New South Wales), Victoria, Western Australia, and South Queensland. As the week went on, discussions took place, and the Australian Women's Soccer Association (AWSA) was born. A national championship was played between 1974 and 1993, which expanded to include a junior version (in 1983) and a youth version (in 1985).

In 1975, the Australian national team was invited to the first Asian Women's Championships in Hong Kong. They didn't have a fully international side, so an unofficial select team played as Australia. In 1978, they were invited to the inaugural World Women's Invitational Tournament in Taiwan. Most national teams didn't have enough money to pay for flights and accommodation at the time, so the Chinese FA met most of these costs. Consequently, the first Australian women's national team was formed.

In New Zealand, football associations formed in Canterbury and Wellington once the ban was lifted in 1971. Two years later, the Northern Women's FA launched a regional league. Other league cups began, and the first international against Australia was played in 1974. The pivotal year for women's football in New Zealand came in 1975 when the Auckland FA was invited to send a team to the first Asian Cup. At the time, there was no national team, but this invitation led to the formation of the New Zealand Women's

Soccer Association and the birth of the first Football Ferns. Roy Cox, now regarded as the father of women's football in New Zealand, began preparations for the inaugural Asian Cup. He was instrumental in forming the Women's Soccer Association and raised funds for the squad so they could compete in the Cup in Hong Kong. Roy both played and coached football and when he put a women's team together at his club in 1973, his wife, Barbara, began to play. She fell in love with the game, along with her teammates. With a squad of 16 players and Barbara as captain, the first Football Ferns played some preparation matches and then flew off to the Asian Cup. They beat Hong Kong and Malaysia in the group stage and then beat local rivals Australia in the semi-finals. In the final, they defeated Thailand and won the first Asian Cup in front of 12,000 spectators.

The following year, 1976, a National Women's Tournament began in New Zealand. The annual event was a week-long tournament at a single venue and featured teams from across the country. Each team played at least once a day to get the fixtures played in a single week, and for the first decade, Wellington and Auckland dominated the event. The tournament ran until 2002 when it became the National Women's Soccer League, now a traditional football league played over a season rather than a week.

Despite their success in the Asian Cup, the national team didn't play again until 1979, when the Trans-Tasman Cup, between them and Australia, was set up to provide the countries with regular international contests.

The United States Women's National Team (USWNT) remains the most successful national women's football team in the world. They've won four World Cups and four Olympic gold medals to date, and they're often considered as having a head start in football. In reality, the U.S. was behind many other countries in terms of development, especially European countries. Their advantage didn't come from starting sooner, but they did have something that other countries didn't have: Title IX.

In 1972, the United States of America passed one of the most significant laws in the fight for equality. On the face of it, a simple law, Title IX, stopped sex discrimination within schools and gave equal access and funding to students of both sexes. The law states "No person in the United States shall, on the basis of sex, be excluded from participation in, be denied the benefits of, or be subjected to discrimination under any education program or activity receiving Federal financial assistance."

The law meant complete equality of education within high schools and colleges, which extended to sport. The effect was to increase the levels of female student athletes dramatically (when Title IX was introduced, 7% of high school athletes were females, but by 2019, 43% were female), and women's college football (soccer in the U.S.) became one of the main beneficiaries of the law.

Crucially, as well as equal access to sport, there also had to be "equal spending on athletic programs". The investment was unprecedented anywhere in the world, and soon, universities were starting soccer programmes for females. In 1979, the University of North Carolina (UNC) started its women's programme under head coach Anson Dorrance. Dorrance is a legend in U.S. women's football. Already the men's team coach at the University of North Carolina, in 1979, his duties expanded to coach the newly formed women's team too. There were no national championships in the U.S. then, so Dorrance and another coach, Chris Lidstone, asked the Association for Intercollegiate Athletics for Women (AIAW) if they'd be interested in forming one. They were, and a U.S. women's college league began.

Two years later, Dorrance's North Colorado Tar Heels won the 1981 AIAW title. The National Collegiate Athletics Association (NCAA), which was uninterested in women's football until that point, changed its mind after the success of the AIAW championships and started an NCAA league. Dorrance's eye for talent has meant the Tar Heels have always had world-class players amongst their ranks, and his teams helped build a strong foundation for the U.S. national team. Despite Title IX being passed in 1972, it took until the end of the decade before college teams were developed, and a national U.S. team was still a few years away.

Years ahead of the U.S., Canada's first unofficial national team formed in 1971. By 1975, the Canadian Women's National Championships were established, which gave teams the chance to compete at a national level. The following year, there were so many girls who wanted to play that the Calgary Minor Soccer Association sponsored the first all-girls tournament in Western Canada. Leagues were set up for girls' teams, and out of this, regional club championships developed across the country in Under-14, Under-16, and Under-18 age groups.

China's football history dates back centuries, but it wasn't until the 1970s that it began to grow and become organised. During the decade, the government started to invest in the game. As a result, there was significant growth, and many teams formed. In 1977, the Republic of China hosted the second edition of the Women's Asian Cup and won it at the first time of asking. By the end of the decade, the first semi-professional women's team had been established in Xi'an. In Japan, the first team formed in 1966 when an elementary school started its first girls' team, but it wasn't until the 1970s that the sport began to take off. The number of players increased, and regional leagues started across the country. In 1977, a Japanese representative team was brought together to play in their first Asian Women's Championship. In 1979, a domestic league cup began: the Empress' Cup. Equivalent to the men's Emperor's Cup, it now includes 36 teams from across the country. The most successful clubs are Nippon TV Tokyo and Verdy Beleza, but it was FC Jinnan who won the first event in 1979.

Football caught on in parts of Africa, too. Official leagues began in Nigeria, but just as in Europe, there was no interest from the male football federation, and it was down to individuals to form teams and organise matches. One of these individuals was a coach named Christopher Akintunde Abisuga, who founded a team in Nigeria named the Sugar Babes Ladies FC. With no female opponents, the teams played against boys' teams and sometimes travelled to different countries for games. As they travelled further afield, they also spread the word about football. In 1978, the Nigeria Female Football Organising Association was set up, although it took another six years before a championship was formed. Regular games were played in Senegal and South Africa too, and later in the decade, leagues formed. In South Africa, at this point, women's football was only played by wealthier women of European ancestry, who were encouraged to challenge the system like their European counterparts. These women helped form the South African Women's Football Association (SAWFA), which in 1979 launched an inter-province tournament for the first time.

By the end of the 1970s, women played football in every corner of the world. When the English FA lifted the ban on their pitches, it sent a signal to other countries, but removing the ban wasn't the same as supporting the development of the game. In England, the opportunities for women to play were still limited and wholly amateur. Opportunities in France and Italy attracted players across to Europe for semi-professional careers, and more major tournaments were organised. Pressure built on UEFA and FIFA to take charge of the women's game and create tournaments of their own. Women's football had shown its promise. Now, it needed to get the backing of the major governing bodies.

8

The 1980s, Part 1: Organisation

A decade after the ban was lifted, and despite the growing number of women playing around the world, neither UEFA nor FIFA had organised a major international tournament. As "unofficial" tournaments continued, UEFA came under enough pressure to force them to begin talking about a European Championships for women.

In February 1980, UEFA met for a conference, and the 18 national associations who attended felt it was time to do everything possible to get the women's game and the potential money-making tournaments under their control. It was time to stop the "wily businessmen" who had so far organised all the major events from making any more money from women's football and to create a UEFA European competition. The UEFA Women's Football Committee was brought back to life, and this time, it had two female members: Patricia Gregory from England and Hannelore Ratzeburg from Germany. In March 1981, UEFA decided it should "start a competition for national representative women teams under the condition that at least 12 national associations will enter a team". With enough interest, the first UEFA Euros could be organised soon.

However, there was no such discussion by FIFA, and a new series of "unofficial" World Cup events were organised throughout the eighties. Ultimately, the decade bridged the gap between the independently organised championships of the seventies and the governing body-backed future of football. The eighties were somewhere in the middle and had both official and unofficial international competitions, with a mixture of the Mundialito World Cups and the first UEFA Euros. Women's football was developing.

The breakthrough of the UEFA European Championships was still a few years off, but there was the first Mundialito (Spanish for "little World Cup") to contest at the beginning of the decade. This prestigious global invitational tournament was organised independently of FIFA. Japan hosted the first edition in September 1981. The tournament was part of their festivities known as "Portopia 81", held in Kobe, Japan. Portopia was a festival to celebrate the opening of a brand new artificial Port Island — any excuse for football. Japan invited Italy, Denmark, and England, and the Japanese FA funded the trips for the visiting nations. Their vision was for the inexperienced Japanese team to learn from the more experienced European teams. Spoiler alert: this long-term plan paid off at the 2011 World Cup. The three European teams flew off to exotic Asian shores for the first Mundialito event, an exciting experience for the teams. The

Mundialito competitions are now considered forerunners to the FIFA World Cup, which was still a decade away.

Mundialito '81 matches were double headers (two games played one after another). The first round was played at the new Port Island in Kobe, but round two was played 300 miles away in Tokyo. England beat Japan but lost to Denmark. Italy beat Japan and drew with Denmark. It isn't known why, but the Japan-Denmark game and the England-Italy games weren't played. It's possible the 9-0 win for Italy over Japan in round two may have played a role. Whatever happened, Italy were declared the winners.

It was the first time an England team had played a side outside of Europe. The players enjoyed the opportunity and posed for photos at Heathrow Airport before their flight; once they landed, they signed autographs for the Japanese fans. WFA chairman David Hunt later took great pride in noting that by going to Japan, the England women's team had done something their male equivalents hadn't. Despite being the first England team to play in Japan, interest from the national media at home was limited. Carol Thomas, who later became England captain, told me,

"There was quite a bit of local interest [around Hull] in the media but virtually nothing in the national press. That was par for the course, but the local stuff was really good."

Although they were breaking boundaries, England's Lionesses were hardly noticed across the country.

In 1984, Italy took over running the Mundialito and hosted the event for the next four editions. The women's federation and the

Italian Olympic Committee joined forces to run the event. A local sports newspaper and major sponsors backed the competition, and again, the organisers met the teams' costs. West Germany, England, and Belgium joined the hosts for the event. Italy won the 1984 Mundialito, led by their non-Italian talisman, Rose Reilly. Getting Rose to play for them was a stroke of genius. Alongside Carolina Morace and Betty Vignotto, Rose scored in the final to beat West Germany 3-1. Rose was named Italy's player of the tournament.

The Mundialito competition continued as a non-FIFA World Cup throughout the decade, but the long-awaited UEFA European Championships had arrived for European countries. The qualification campaign began in 1982, and between August 1982 and October 1983, four groups of four teams battled it out to claim a spot at the very first UEFA championship finals. Groups were allocated by geographical region, so teams from each part of Europe played each other.

Group 1 was Northern Europe and included Sweden, Norway, Finland, and Iceland; Group 2 was England, Scotland, Northern Ireland, and the Republic of Ireland; Group 3 was Southern Europe with Italy, France, Switzerland, and Portugal; and Group 4 was Central Europe made up of Denmark, the Netherlands, West Germany, and Belgium. Games were played over two 35-minute halves with a size four ball. Only the top team in each group qualified for the final main tournament, which then consisted of just two semi-finals and a final. This meant only four teams played in the first UEFA European Championships finals: Sweden, England, Italy, and Denmark.

There was no single host country in the early UEFA Euros, and the semi-finals were played over a home leg and an away leg. In the semi-finals, England drew Denmark, one of the tournament favourites. England captain Carol Thomas described it for me,

"In April, we played the two legs of the semi-final against Denmark just three weeks apart, winning both legs. That was a bit of a shock as Denmark were considered the team of the tournament, but we were good over those two legs, and I was so proud of the team, the individuals, and the two performances. Indeed, the Danish Press headlines for their 2nd leg loss read as: 'Kvinderne fik EM-fiasko', 'Women fail to make European Championship fiasco'. But we were good on that day, with virtually no shots on our goal."

It was a great start for the early Lionesses, first Euros competition, first final. In the other semi-final, Sweden beat Italy.

The final between England and Sweden was again played over two legs. The first leg was played less than two weeks after the second leg of the semi-final, in May 1984. The first leg was played in Sweden, and Carol Thomas described the team as "nervous but confident of our abilities". She described the experience for me:

"The first leg in Sweden was in the Ullevi, their national stadium, in front of 6,000+ spectators. It was warm, sunny and a playing surface well worthy of a European final. It had mass national media coverage, papers, radio, and the whole game was beamed live on TV. I think it fair to say the performance was a backs-to-the-wall job, but we kept them to a 1-0 defeat which ironically, we can now look back on as a victory of sorts. I think it reflected perfectly the work ethic of the whole squad, to work hard, fight hard individually, defend as a team, and leave everything on the pitch. The Swedish media headlines were all about Pia Sundhage's bullet header of a goal, but I did make a goal-line clearance late in the game and I still believe that clearance kept us in the tie. However, our overall performance on that day sent an element of caution to the Swedish and it left their manager, Ulf Lyfors, to say in one newspaper headline: '1-0 det racker inte langt', '1-0, it's not enough'. I think he had seen that we were wounded Lionesses, and there's nothing more dangerous than a wounded animal."

Carol described the return leg at Kenilworth Road, Luton, as "the polar opposite of Sweden", calling it "the Battle of Kenilworth Bog".

"No media, no papers, no radio, and only a TV Start-Up company that didn't survive much beyond that final. Little FA interest, no Wembley or big London club ground, and 48 hours of torrential rain prior to a game that was eventually played on a grassless Kenilworth Road, mud bath. If it had been a men's game, it most definitely would have been called off. But we still felt we could win. We had a fair crowd for us, of just over 2,500. Sure enough, we took the upper hand and went into the lead and despite throwing everything at them, we didn't manage to add to our tally. The two-legged final had finished 1-1 on aggregate. It was decided that no extra time was to be played. I don't think the pitch could have taken it anyway, and so it was straight to penalties. England and penalties are not a match made in heaven and so the Swedes ran out victors winning 4-3 on penalties. Defeated but not shamed, and it is only when you realise, we were the first senior England team (men or women) to reach a European final, that it hits you."

The next day, Carol Thomas was the first England women's player to be interviewed on national TV when she appeared on BBC Breakfast. But despite more national media coverage than they'd had before, it's hard not to think about what could have been if they'd had more support: "I think the most disappointing thing is what could have happened had we had full FA backing from that point on. We were one of the best teams in Europe, if not the world. With the right investment of time, resources, and money, just think what could have been achieved in the following years, not just for my generation but all the subsequent generations of international players."

[Author note: What's poignant for me is that in 1984, I was just falling in love with football. Carol Thomas would have been my role model and idol. Instead, all I saw was men playing, so Bryan Robson was my hero. No disrespect to Bryan (Captain Marvel); he was a worthy idol for a young girl, but we can see now how girls having female players to look up to changes everything. Instead of feeling I was the only girl in the world who played football, I'd have seen the opportunity to continue playing. It's powerful.]

A 17-year-old Hope Powell — future England manager — was also part of the team for the final in 1984, and watched the penalties from the halfway line. She once described the state of the pitch as "absolutely shocking" and said, "The ball kept getting stuck in the mud or pools of water, and the penalty areas were very difficult."

It may have been a Euro final, but it was a long way away from a perfect Wembley pitch.

The tournaments came thick and fast, and 1985 brought the next Mundialito. This time, the U.S. joined England, Italy, and Denmark. This team was the very first U.S. women's national football team. The U.S. Soccer Federation wanted to test their players against European sides and chose a select team of college players to become the first official national team. They entered the Mundialito in Italy, knowing it was a prestigious tournament and knowing the best nations in the world competed in it. They wanted to find out how much work they had to do to compete with the best.

In their second Mundialito match (also their second-ever match), Michelle Akers scored their first-ever goal. They lost three out of four of their games but got a draw against Denmark. They had also created a major star of the game; Michelle Akers became one of the greatest players in history.

The 1985 Mundialito World Cup was won for the first time by England. It was their first major international trophy. This team of Lionesses didn't get the recognition they would now but were an extremely successful side. Their captain, Carol Thomas, said in July 2017,

"From 1974 to 1985, we were the most successful England Women's Team. Not only did we win the Home International Championship in 1976, we went on to 4th place in the 1979 unofficial European Cup, runners-up in the 1984 European

Profile: Carol Thomas

Carol kicked a ball as soon as she could walk. But it was after watching the 1966 World Cup that she began taking it seriously. Her first competitive game, aged 11, was playing for the works team British Oil and Cocoa Mills in Yorkshire. Her talent was spotted and she moved to Reckitts Ladies, where she worked under Flo Bilton. In 1974, aged 19, Carol won her first England cap. Within two years, she was the first choice right back and was made captain at the age of 20. Carol led the team to win the 1976 Pony Home International, to a runners-up medal at the first UEFA Euros in 1984, and to their first Mundialito win in 1985. She captained their first official tournament outside of Europe at the 1981 Portopia Festival in Japan.

She was captain for nine years — the longest-serving captain until Faye White overtook her in 2011.

During her 56 caps, she was the most successful England captain until the current Lionesses. Despite temporarily retiring to become a mum in 1993, she later returned to playing locally and only fully retired at age 54. She still occasionally plays and recently had a go at walking football ("It's really hard to walk!"). Carol is an unsung hero of the modern game. In 2021, she was inducted into the National Football Museum's Hall of Fame.

Championship, and winners of the 1985 Mundialito, thereby becoming World Champions (with many of that squad going on to win the 1988 Mundialito). Comparisons with the modern era would be unfair. You only compete in your own time."

She told me how she feels about her England team's place in history.

"We were breaking down barriers and moving the game, inch by inch, into the mainstream. I hear that the current players are breaking down glass ceilings, and that is brilliant recognition. But I do think that we moved the earth above and then broke down the concrete structures that hid those glass ceilings. I always like to say that my generation was just one of those stepping stones to what the Lionesses get now, and I get immense pleasure and pride out of that."

She is right. As I hope this book shows, all the steps were and are vital in moving the game forward.

Carol Thomas led England in six tournaments, won two of them, and was a runner-up in another. She was the first woman to 50 England caps, the youngest captain, the first player to captain England 50 times, and the first women's captain to win a major trophy (when England beat Italy in the final of the 1985 Mundialito World Cup). She was the first captain (man or woman) to reach a senior Euro final. As she says,

"It is a record I am incredibly proud of, and it can never be taken away from me .... unless history is rewritten!"

[Author note: When I wrote to Carol to ask about her experiences, I mentioned it made me sad for both of us that I didn't know about her and her successful England team when I was a girl falling in love with football. I also said I felt a little ashamed that I'd never thought to find out more about the history before now. She very wisely replied,

"Never underestimate the contribution you made, albeit small. The fact you played with your male peers down the local park in 1984, pre the FA takeover of the game, will have opened their (your male peers) minds to the fact women/girls can play football and that some can be pretty good at it. That will have made it just that little bit easier for those that followed. Indeed, did any of the daughters of those male peers go on to play football? Go on to be football referees, administrators, etc, etc?".

I'm welling up as I type that and maybe I get a slight sense of pride that I was a tiny part of the journey. Perhaps you were too?]

The Mundialito was held again in 1986, and with the growth in popularity, the competition was expanded to six international teams. Newcomers Japan, China, Mexico, and Brazil (where football had only recently become legal for women) joined Italy and the U.S. this time. Only a year after making their debut, the U.S. team reached the final but finished runners-up to Italy. There was no Mundialito in 1987, and with a possible FIFA World Cup on the horizon, the 1988 Mundialito was the last time it was held. Italy, the U.S., West Germany, France, and England took part, and England lifted their second World Cup trophy. It was the end of an era, but it cannot be overstated how important the Italian-organised tournaments were in steering the game through the previous decades. Italy's dual contributions of a domestic league that treated players as professionals and the organisation of international tournaments propelled and grew women's football across the world.

In Europe, unofficial and official tournaments weaved across the international schedule, and in 1987, the second UEFA Euro event was held. England, Italy, Norway, and Sweden qualified to compete in the main tournament, which was held in a single host country for the first time. Norway had a home advantage as hosts and beat Italy in front of a crowd of 5,000 spectators; England lost to Sweden in front of 300 people. Norway beat Sweden in the final and won their first UEFA Euros. Meanwhile, pressure had been mounting on FIFA to organise a World Cup event.

Profile: Michelle Akers

Michelle Akers was the first modern superstar of women's football. Born in 1966, the physical and aggressive forward played her college football (soccer) with the University of Central Florida between 1985 and 1988. She became their all-time leading goal scorer with 52 goals and recorded 30 assists. During this time, the U.S. women's national team played their first international match against Italy at the 1985 Mundialito. Michelle was part of the squad but couldn't play the first game because of an ankle injury. She made up for lost time in the second match and scored the United States Women's National Team's (USWNT) first international goal, against Denmark. She continued to score for the USWNT over the next 15 years and finished with 107 goals from 155 matches. At the time of writing, she is still sixth on the USWNT all-time goalscorer list. In 2002, she was named FIFA Female Player of the Century alongside China's Sun Wen. In 2004, Pelé named Michelle Akers on his list of 125 greatest living players as part of FIFA's 100th anniversary celebrations. She was inducted into the U.S. National Soccer Hall of Fame in 2004.

Some of that pressure came from Norwegian delegate Ellen Wille, who, after the 1986 Mundialito, became the first woman to address the FIFA Congress. She demanded the governing body take note of women's football and lobbied for a women's

World Cup and an Olympic football tournament. Unsurprisingly, most of the male delegates weren't interested, but then FIFA president João Havelange backed her up. He suggested a trial event to see if there was enough interest in a women's World Cup. Consequently, in 1988, China hosted the FIFA Women's Invitation Tournament.

This dress rehearsal for the FIFA World Cup took place in Guangdong, China, in the first two weeks of June 1988. Twelve teams from the six football confederations across the world took part: China, Canada, Côte d'Ivoire, Netherlands, Australia, Brazil, Norway, Thailand, Czechoslovakia, Japan, Sweden, and the United States took part. [Side note: Among the Netherlands team was 18-year-old Sarina Weigman]. Norway, Brazil, Sweden, and China reached the semi-finals, and Norway beat Sweden 1-0 to win the tournament. Linda Medalen of Norway scored the winning goal of the FIFA World Cup test event. In total, twenty-six games were played across four cities, and 81 goals were scored. The final attracted a crowd of around 30,000 people, and the tournament was hailed as a success. A few weeks later, FIFA announced that the first official FIFA Women's World Cup would take place in 1991.

[Author note: I remember the 1988 men's Euros well. The Dutch men were incredible during this Euros campaign (and won the trophy). But I had no idea there was a women's World Cup test tournament in the same year. The park behind our house was my pitch growing up, with trees as the goal at one end and jumpers for goalposts at the other. I distinctly remember a game of headers and volleys (my favourite) with my male mates. I scored a cracking volley (I can see it now) and wheeled away in celebration, pretending I was Marco van Basten. To think, I could have been Sarina Weigman.]

West Germany hosted the 1989 UEFA Euros and won their first title. It's interesting to see how the fanbase has developed over the years, and the average attendance per game was an impressive 8,875. Over the tournament, 35,500 people came to watch, and 22,000 watched the final between West Germany and Norway, showing the interest in Germany.

The international tournaments gave a rough overview of how football was developing, but how did that translate to the league organisation needed to truly grow women's football?

Profile: Sun Wen

China's Sun Wen is one of the greatest players in history. Born in 1973, she began playing 10 years later; she was inspired by her dad, who took her to matches. Her senior career began in 1989 as a forward for Shanghai. During over 650 appearances, she scored 164 goals.

She made her debut for China in 1990. During her career, she scored 106 goals in 152 games and went to four World Cups. She captained her country in the watershed 1999 World Cup final. At the tournament, Sun Wen won a rare double, picking up the Golden Ball (best player) and Golden Boot (with seven goals). Following a silver medal at the 1996 Olympics and second place at the 1999 World Cup, Sun Wen moved to Atlanta Beat in the U.S. She returned to China in 2003 to prepare for the World Cup. During four World Cups and two Olympics, Sun Wen played 28 matches and scored 16 goals, but unfortunately didn't win either major trophy. In 2000, alongside Michelle Akers, Sun Wen was voted FIFA Women's Player of the Century.

Profile: Linda Medalen

Linda Medalen was one of Norway's best players. She played her club football in Norway with Asker Fotball and in the Japanese league for Nikko. During 152 appearances for Norway, she scored 64 goals. As her career progressed, she moved from forward to midfielder to defender — a versatile player. Her international debut came in 1987; she scored her first goals (2) at the 1988 World Cup test event, including the winner in the final. Medalen's goal in the first minute of Norway's semi-final against Sweden in the 1989 Euros helped them into the final. In 1991 FIFA World Cup, Medalen scored six goals, including two in their semi-final win and an equaliser in the final against the U.S. On the way to winning the 1993 Euros and 1995 World Cup, Linda scored two goals and had three assists. At the 1996 Olympics, she was joint top scorer. Medalen captained Norway to the 1999 World Cup but injury kept her out of the 2000 Olympics. The Norwegian Football Federation withdrew her funding soon after her injury. Linda retired in 2006, aged 41. During her career, she helped Norway win the 1988 World Cup trial event, the 1993 Euros, the 1995 World Cup, and a bronze medal at the 1996 Olympics.

9

The 1980s, Part 2: The Game Evolves

Europe

The Women's Football Association (WFA) in England opened its first proper administration office in 1981. Volunteers mostly ran the organisation, and under their direction, football grew and developed. In May 1984, the FA decided it was time to take more responsibility, and the WFA came under the umbrella of the English Football Association for the first time. This meant the WFA was treated like a County FA, still running itself, but with access to the central FA support system and finances.

As I mentioned in the previous chapter, although the Lionesses were successful internationally during the 1980s, their success was virtually invisible in their home country. This meant club football was invisible too. There were pockets of teams for girls and young women to play in, many based in the north east of England where support for female players was stronger, but you had to know they were there. Ex-England player Issy Pollard's story typifies women's football during the 1980s and 1990s. Issy's football journey began in the 1980s in a tiny village in West Yorkshire. As soon as she could walk, she kicked a ball around. But even in the more football-friendly north east, getting into a team was a combination of determination and luck. Fortunately, Issy had an ally in her school headmaster.

"My headmaster at the time, I think my mum ended up phoning him to see if I could be part of the boys' team. I remember him, I can see the vision now, we were having lunch, and he came and knelt down beside me and put his arm around me and said, 'We'd love to have you on the team' he was just really, really encouraging. To actually play on a team at junior school was great. And so that was the start of it."

From there, Issy's mum contacted the WFA and found her nearest club team, Bradford City. Issy was 11 or 12 and describes Bradford City as "a great entry into football". From there, she moved to Bronte, another local club, where they had an international player, Clare Taylor. With the backing of her international teammate, Issy found herself part of the England set-up at age 16. There were no scouts everywhere looking for talented girls at that time; for most girls, progress was down to being in the right place at the right time.

[Author note: Issy's story is another poignant parallel for me, as Issy and I are the same age. What would have happened if my head teacher had let me play on the school team? I think my mates advocated that I was good enough (I'm forever grateful to those boys who never questioned why I was playing and always let me join in), but I guess we never thought to challenge it further. At

that time, football for girls involved luck. If you were lucky enough
to have a teacher who supported you, you stood a chance. If not,
you couldn't be in a team. But maybe the right people got the
chances; Issy was clearly much more adventurous than I was.]

Much of the visibility of women's football in the north east was
thanks to Doncaster Rovers Belles. Donny Belles (as they were
affectionately known) were formed nearly two decades earlier, in
1969, and had been dominant throughout the 1970s. They began
when a group of women, including Sheila Stocks, who sold the
"Golden Goal tickets" for Doncaster Rovers men's team, decided
they wanted a team of their own. The Belle Vue Belles formed
(named after their home ground, Belle Vue) and later became
known as the Doncaster Rovers Belles, Donny Belles, or simply the
Belles. In 1983, they won their first WFA Cup and were involved
in six of the Cup finals throughout the decade (they won three of
them). The Belles were dominant through the seventies and into
the eighties and improved the profile of the game in the north
east and across the country. Their dominance was only challenged
when a new London team came along. A team that, along with
Donny Belles, would raise the standards of football and provide an
exciting rivalry for the foreseeable future. That team was Arsenal.

Having male allies speeds up the rate of change in football. In
the 1980s in England, the most influential ally and driver of
change was Vic Akers. Vic founded Arsenal Ladies in 1987, and
throughout his 22 years as manager, he supported his players,
introduced professionalism into an amateur sport, and drove
the standard of women's football up across England. He also

established Arsenal as a dominant force in domestic football. Arsenal Ladies won their first trophy, the Premier League Cup, in 1992. The following year they cleaned up, winning a domestic treble. Throughout his long career with Arsenal, Akers won three domestic trebles, 12 Premier League titles, 10 FA Cups and 10 League Cups. In 2007, Arsenal were the first (and so far, only) English team to win all three domestic trophies plus the UEFA Women's Cup (now the Champion's League).

What made Vic Akers and his Arsenal team so successful? Vic was totally committed to his team. It was an era when the game in England was completely amateur. To avoid players being distracted and to help them commit to the team, Vic found them jobs around the club so they could support themselves and remain in the football environment. He also made them feel like professionals on the pitch, carefully planning his drills to get the best out of the players. By committing himself to their wellbeing and football careers, he, in return, got commitment from his players. He was professional in his approach to the game because his main aim was to grow the club and win trophies. His professional approach to tactics, scouting, training, and the financial aspects of the club were way ahead of the time. His planning worked, and Arsenal became the best in the game when it came to equality and professionalism.

In the 1980s and 1990s, the rivalry between Arsenal and Donny Belles helped spark slightly more interest in the game. But a general lack of visibility meant that, aside from a few more fans at pitches, most people didn't know women played football at these levels. As a young girl in the 1980s, I had no idea there were idols for me to look up to. I had no idea other females were as passionate about the game as I was. That could have changed a lot for girls like me. As the decade ended, though, this lack of visibility began changing in England when, 19 years after the Women's FA Cup was first held, highlights were shown on television for the first time.

In 1989, Channel 4 showed televised highlights of the game for the first time. The programme wasn't aired until the day after the final, but for the first time, women's football appeared on English national television. Manchester United's Old Trafford hosted the first televised final between Leasowe Pacific (who became Everton Ladies in 1995) and Friends of Fulham (London), both major clubs at the time. Leasowe won 3-2 and lifted the trophy. Fulham's goals were both scored by someone who later changed women's football in England: Hope Powell. According to some sources, the television audience for the first Women's FA Cup highlights programme was nearly two million people.

Women's football didn't really develop in the rest of the British Isles. The Scottish national team suffered from the lack of FA support, and Wales only played ten international fixtures during the entire decade, and only then because Sylvia Gore (an ex-England player) bankrolled and managed the team for several years.

The Republic of Ireland played their first competitive international match in 1982, and the same year, Northern Ireland toured the USA. However, there was little meaningful development across the rest of the decade.

It was very different in Italy, though, where women could earn money playing football. Understandably, this attracted talented players. The Italian's passion for football of any kind brought famous names from all over Europe to their country, including Pia Sundhage from Sweden, Kerry Davis from England, and Rose Reilly from Scotland. Italy was the centre of women's football during the eighties, boasting homegrown stars like Carolina Morace as well as importing the world's best players.

Profile: Kerry Davis

Kerry Davis made her debut in 1982 and was the first black woman to play for England. She was a crucial attacking force for 16 years and became their top scorer. She scored twice in her first game, a qualifier for the 1984 Euros. Two weeks later, Kerry scored all four goals in England's next qualifier, against Scotland. Out of six qualification games, Kerry scored in five, netting a total of 11 times. In 1984, during the first leg of the Euros semi-final against Denmark, Kerry scored again but, unfortunately, couldn't repeat it in the final. Kerry played all four of England's matches at the 1995 World Cup. Due to her versatility, she often played in midfield. Kerry had scored 44 goals in 82 games for England, a record that stood until Kelly Smith beat it in 2012 (the record was beaten again in 2021 by Ellen White).
During her club career, Kerry played for Crewe Alexandra Ladies before signing for Italian club Roi Lazio. She played for Trani 80 and Napoli in Italy, before returning to Crewe. She played in the FA Cup Final in 1994 for Knowsley United (later Liverpool) before finishing her career with Croydon. During her time at Croydon, she won the league and cup double, her first domestic trophies.

Profile: Carolina Morace

Carolina began playing senior football in 1978 and became one of
Italy's top strikers. In the 1984/85 Serie A season, she was top scorer
for Lazio and went on to win the accolade for 11 consecutive seasons
(for various teams). She was the first woman to score a hat-trick at the
FIFA Women's World Cup when she scored four in a game at the 1991
competition. During 153 appearances for her country, Carolina scored
105 goals.

She retired from playing in 1998. She began coaching with Lazio's
women's team in 1998. In 1999, she became the first female to coach
a professional men's team when she took charge of Viterbese (who
played in Serie C1) in June 1999. Unfortunately, this huge stride
forward for equality was snuffed out when Carolina resigned after only
two matches because the club's president interfered in the running of
the team. She coached the Italian women's national side between
2000 and 2005, when they twice qualified for the Euros. Carolina also
coached the Canadian women's national team, Trinidad and Tobago,
and then went back to Italy to head up Milan and then Lazio.

Germany also began taking football seriously during this decade.
Their first women's club knockout cup began in 1981, and they
played their first official international in 1982. Women's cup finals
were played as double-headers ahead of the men's cup finals,
which brought bigger audiences. Regional leagues spread further
across the country in the middle of the decade and in 1989, West
Germany hosted the Euros, demonstrating their commitment
to developing the sport. By winning the Euros this year, they
kick-started a period of domination in Europe. In contrast, the
French Football Federation remained unsupportive of the French

national team during the 1980s. Consequently, the team struggled to make an impact on the international scene. Reims, who had supplied much of the national team until now, began to fade away and France failed to qualify for the final stages of the Euros throughout the decade.

The Spanish FA now began to recognise women's football for the first time, and a national club cup competition was started. A national team started, too, but when they were invited to play at the 1981 Mundialito, the governing body stopped them. Spain's national team finally played their first official international in 1983, and their first domestic league championship began in 1988.

Sweden has a strong history of gender equality, and in the early 1970s, the country actively addressed the issue politically. By actively seeking equality, women in football were given opportunities that helped them rise to the top of the game. The football association hired a full-time professional coach for the national side in 1980 when Ulf Lyfors took charge. [Side note: Sweden's support for women's football was a long way ahead of England, who only appointed Hope Powell as their first full-time coach eighteen years later, in 1998.] In 1982, the first woman officiated in Sweden's top women's league, which put their female referees at the front of the game, too. Domestically, Sweden's first women's league began in 1988 and was semi-professional from the start. The Damallsvenskan remains their premier league and has played host to some of the world's top footballers over the years, including Brazil's Marta (who arrived at age 18 and developed into the world's best player whilst there), Hope Solo (who later won the World Cup with the U.S.), Anja Mittag (who won one World Cup, two Euros, and an Olympic gold medal with Germany), and legendary U.S. player Michelle Akers, amongst many others. The Damaalsvenskan provided a haven for players from all over the globe whose own countries didn't value their sport.

Norway was growing its football foundations, too. Like in Sweden, a desire to strive for gender equality developed women's football alongside men's. Local and regional leagues formed across Norway, and in 1984, their First Division (now Toppserien) was established. In 1987, Norway won the Euros. Finland's development was slower than its neighbours but followed a similar path. During the eighties, the Finnish Football Association formed a women's committee to help develop the game. Collaboration between the Finnish FA and Finnish schools meant they had a pathway to bring more girls into the sport, and in 1985, the first national competition for schools was organised. Buoyed by this, the number of girls playing exceeded the number of women playing for the first time in 1986.

For many European nations, there was some degree of progress across this decade. As West Germany and Sweden pushed things forward in Europe, arguably the most important team — in terms of world football progress — was just getting started.

Profile: Pia Sundhage

Pia Sundhage has been successful as a player and a coach. Born in 1960, Pia debuted for Sweden aged 15, and became their top scorer. She was also top scorer at the 1984 Euros, which Sweden won. A few years later, her image appeared on a postage stamp. She played at the 1991 and 1995 FIFA World Cups and the 1996 Olympics. She scored the first goal in a women's match at Wembley when Sweden beat England 2-0 in 1989. She reached 146 caps and scored 71 goals. Pia's coaching career began in the Swedish league, but in 2001, she moved to the U.S. to become assistant coach at Philadelphia Charge. She then became head coach at Boston Breakers, where they won the league title. She became assistant coach for China in 2007 before becoming head coach of the U.S. team. They won Olympic gold at Beijing in 2008 and London in 2012. In 2011, they reached the World Cup final, their first since the 1999 win. Pia stepped down in 2012 for her dream job as head coach of Sweden. They reached the semi-finals of the 2013 Euros, Round of 16 at the 2015 World Cup, and won a silver medal at the Rio Olympics. She briefly coached Brazil and currently coaches Switzerland.

The Rest of the World

Unburdened by historic gender stereotypes in football (because men mostly played American football rather than "soccer"), the U.S. women were able to carve out their own place in the sport. Although the passing of Title IX in 1972 meant education programmes had to fund women's sport equally to men, it took another decade before the introduction of the first annual tournament. In 1982, the National Collegiate Athletics Association (NCAA) Women's Soccer Tournament, was born. In

1985, the U.S. Soccer Federation asked coach Mike Ryan to bring together a squad of their best college players to form a national side to compete in the 1985 Mundialito tournament in Italy. This became the first U.S. Women's National Team (USWNT), handpicked to take on some of the best teams in Europe in their first international matches. The USA's intent was shown right there. At the 1985 Mundialito tournament, they were students of the game; soon, they would be masters. Although they lost every match, the experience was invaluable at their first tournament. In 1986, they played their first home international (against Canada), and Anson Dorrance became the team's first full-time head coach (again, years ahead of England). His target was to create a team that would be competitive at the 1986 Mundialito and beyond. He smashed it. The team beat China, Brazil, and Japan in the tournament and finished as runners-up to Italy. Only one year after their international debut, they came second in a World Cup: an ominous sign of things to come for the rest of the world.

By the end of the decade, the U.S. had taken part in the World Cup test event in 1988 and qualified for the first-ever FIFA-endorsed Women's World Cup, due to take place in 1991. The national team, set up only a few years ago, was about to take over the football world. Title IX showed what equal sports funding can help achieve, and, ultimately, the influence of the USWNT's success spread throughout the world, driving standards up everywhere.

In Canada, things were, unfortunately, different. The Canadian women had to fight continuously for every scrap of funding for their national team. In 1982, the Canadian Soccer Association (CSA) officially recognised women's soccer but provided very little support. In 1986, the first official national team was formed, but the CSA had no interest and seemed to hope it would go away. Head coach Neil Turnbull was told that the national programme would be stopped before it had really started if they lost both of their two opening internationals against the U.S. Not the words of a supportive governing body. Canada lost the first game, but fortunately, the Canadians' fight and spirit helped them win the second match, 2-1: much to the irritation of the CSA, I imagine. Canada had scored their first international goals, both of which came from Geri Donelly. At the point of their first internationals, Canada's playing level was the same as the U.S., but when the U.S. invested in football development, Canada got left behind.

After a lengthy legal ban in Brazil, the National Sports Council reinstated sport for women in 1979. In 1981, the first recorded women's beach football tournament took place on Copacabana Beach in Rio de Janeiro. One of the best teams was the local team, EC Radar. In 1982, they switched to football on grass pitches and dominated early state championships. EC Radar represented Brazil at the 1986 Mundialito and played their first official international against the United States. They lost 2-1 to the U.S. but earned their first group stage point with a draw against China. They were unlucky not to qualify for the semi-final stage, which was decided on a coin toss when the group finished with Brazil and China level. Two years later, EC Radar represented Brazil in the test event for the FIFA Women's World Cup and came third out of 12 teams.

In Oceania, Australia and New Zealand continued to contest their three-match series. In 1982, the Oceania Women's Football Confederation was born. In 1983, they set up the Oceania Women's Championship (now known as the Women's Nations Cup). New Caledonia (I know, I had to look it up, too. It's a French territory made up of many South Pacific islands) hosted the first championship. New Zealand, Australia, Fiji, and New Caledonia competed, and New Zealand won. In 1985, the New Zealand WFA set up a World Cup committee to promote the game, and in 1987 a milestone was reached when they beat the United States for the first time. [Side note: a mother and daughter pairing formed part of New Zealand's defence.] Meanwhile, Australia reached the quarter-finals of the 1988 World Cup test event in China.

After restarting their involvement in women's football in the previous decade, China got up and running quickly. They won the Women's Asian Cup three times during the decade, the first time in 1980. In 1981, their first national club competition took place in Chuxiong City, and the next year, a national invitational tournament for the whole of China began. In the mid-1980s, women's football came under the control of the Chinese Football Association, and in 1986, the national team played against the United States for the first time (losing 2-1). The same year, the team travelled to Europe for matches, and an under-16s team was formed. Domestically, things were improving too, and a national league began. In 1988, FIFA chose China to host the test event for the Women's World Cup, a huge boost for football in the country.

Football in Japan also came alive in the 1980s. In March 1980, the first national club championship began. The Empress' Cup (mirroring the men's Emperor's Cup) took place over two days at the Mitsubishi Yowa Soccer Club in Sugamo. Eight teams made up of eight players played out the tournament on a smaller-than-normal pitch. FC Jinnan, who had previously represented Japan in the 1977 Asian Championships, won the first title. In 1981, a full national Japan team was put together for the Asian Football Confederation's (AFC) women's championships. Held in Hong Kong, it cost the players money to travel to the event, but they recorded their first-ever goal there when 16-year-old Etsuko Handa scored the winner against Indonesia. The Japanese FA appointed a qualified coach to run the national team in 1986, a big development if you consider the 1981 team had a schoolteacher coaching them. With a more professional outlook, Japan came second at the Asian Championships. By the end of the decade, a national league had been set up. The Nadeshiko League, as it was named, is still going today and provides the second tier of football in Japan.

Football in Africa was initially driven by Nigeria's Princess Bola Jegede, who set up the first national women's championship in 1984. After the popular National Sports Festival in Nigeria added women's football for the first time in 1989, interest grew, and more teams formed. Soon, there were 28 active clubs in Nigeria, including the Jegede Babes, founded by the Princess. She continued to support and fund football in Nigeria and financed the first women's tournament in 1990, this time with the support of the Nigerian FA (although more moral support than financial support, it seems).

What a decade. By the end of the 1980s, there was clear development in football for women. Across the world, more and more females took part, and now Europe (the leaders of world football at the time) had the UEFA Euros. Football was still virtually invisible in England, but it was being taken more seriously in other countries across the world. The addition of the United States into the football landscape shouldn't be underestimated, and the promise of a FIFA Women's World Cup showed the gatekeepers of football that women's football could no longer be ignored.

10

The 1990s: Icons Assemble

The 1990s began to bring the sport onto the radar of more people. It was the decade FIFA finally cottoned on to the growing popularity and held its first Women's World Cup. And it was the decade that ended with the 1999 United States-hosted watershed World Cup that set new attendance records, had massive worldwide viewing figures, and created stars of the U.S. team. It also helped inspire countless girls and women across the planet. The nineties showed everyone just how popular women's sport could be.

In most countries, we were still decades away from professional football, but the era of the Spice Girls meant girl power was on the rise. We spoke out more loudly about equality, but the battle to change attitudes continued.

Major Tournaments

It may not have been brought to the world's attention, but in 1991, the first FIFA Women's World Cup took place. It was a massive moment for everyone who had ever been involved in women's football. FIFA, however, wasn't convinced they were onto a winner. To protect their World Cup brand, they didn't even call it a "World Cup". What they did call it was possibly the wordiest tournament title of all time: The 1st FIFA World Championship for Women's Football for the M&M's Cup. Wow. M&M's Cup after the sponsor, and it's anyone's guess how they came up with the rest. They later retrospectively named it the 1991 FIFA Women's World Cup.

In November 1991, twelve teams from six confederations travelled to the region of China that had hosted the successful test event. Forty-eight teams entered the qualification process, and each confederation used their regional championship as a qualification event. In Europe, that meant the Euros. The twelve qualifiers were split into three groups: Group A was China, Norway, Denmark, and New Zealand; Group B was the U.S., Sweden, Brazil, and Japan; and Group C was Germany, Italy, Chinese Taipei, and Nigeria. At this point, women still played 80-minute matches.

The games were well attended, and according to the post-tournament technical report, most of them attracted an audience of between 10,000 and 27,000 people. Interest peaked when China, the host nation, played, and 65,000 watched the opening game between China and Norway. Sweden, Norway, Germany, and the U.S. reached the semi-finals (new tournament, same teams in the latter stages). Germany, who had won the Euros for the second time, couldn't do the double and were knocked out in the semi-finals by a dominant U.S. team. On the other side of the draw, Norway convincingly beat Sweden. The first FIFA World

Cup final was played at Tianhe Stadium, Guangzhou, in front of 63,000 spectators. The U.S. beat Norway 2-1 to lift the first FIFA Women's World Cup.

The United States had only played their first international match 16 years ago but were now confirmed as the world's best. With a host of stars and an enviable strike force, the U.S. began their dominance. The legendary Michelle Akers was the top scorer in the 1991 tournament with a staggering ten goals, including the two winning goals in the final. In total, 99 goals were scored in 26 matches. Akers was awarded the Golden Shoe (later renamed the Golden Boot) for scoring the most tournament goals. The Golden Ball, given to the tournament's best player, was awarded to another U.S. striker, Carin Jennings. The first FIFA-sanctioned Women's World Cup was a success and a major milestone in women's football. FIFA was convinced to drop the lengthy name and bestowed their "World Cup" brand on future events.

[Author note: around the same time as the first FIFA Women's World Cup, I was able to choose my preferred PE (physical education) "option" at school. Every few weeks, we could pick a different sport to try and, for the very first time (probably after some nagging), girls could choose a few weeks of football, albeit played on the tennis courts. We were legitimately able to play football for the first time. With the guidance of an actual PE teacher. This was progress. Except it wasn't, not really. I remember the first session. I was excited. This was what I'd been dreaming of. There weren't many girls in the lesson; some were better than others, but we had all chosen to play football. Unfortunately, in those days, some male PE teachers were sexist, or maybe we were just unlucky. In any case, our teacher spent the lesson sneering at the idea of girls playing football. Not coaching us, encouraging us, empowering us, but putting us down. Instead of the anticipated joy, I felt angry, sad, and disappointed. Those weeks were not the dream I had hoped for.]

The Euros continued to occur every two years until the end of the decade before the schedule was altered to make space for the FIFA World Cup. Norway won the Euros in 1993 and Germany won again in 1995. The main Euros championship continued to consist of just semi-finals and a final. Perhaps more important here in terms of the growth and development of the game was the difference in attendance figures depending on where matches were hosted. England hosted a semi-final against Germany at Vicarage Road, Watford, and attracted a crowd of 800 people. The reverse fixture in Germany at the Ruhrstadion, Bochum, attracted a 7,000-strong crowd. Nearly ten times as many spectators came out in Germany compared with England: I think this shows the gulf in how football was being approached in the two countries. Somewhat strangely, the single-leg final between Germany and Sweden was played in Germany, giving them a home advantage: something Germany didn't need. Germany won 3-2 in front of 8,500 fans and picked up their third Euros trophy.

Sweden hosted the second FIFA Women's World Cup in 1995. FIFA committed to calling it the "1995 FIFA Women's World Cup" this time, happy to use its branding after two successful previous events.

Again, 12 teams from six confederations took part, and 54
teams were whittled down to Australia, Brazil, Canada, China,
Denmark, England, Germany, Japan, Nigeria, Norway, Sweden,
and the U.S. UEFA held a separate qualifying competition for the
World Cup (rather than the Euros) this time and England made
their first official appearance.

Other debutants were Australia and Canada. Germany, England,
Sweden, China, Japan, the U.S., Norway, and Denmark advanced
to the quarter-finals. If you're an England fan, have a guess who
England drew for their quarter-final? Yep, Germany. A long and
traditional football rivalry, which had started in the men's game,
was to continue in the women's game too. Somewhat predictably,
Germany beat England and were joined by China, the U.S., and
Norway in the semi-finals. Norway and Germany contested the
final, and Norway finished as World Champions in front of over
17,000 people in Solna. For the first time, a woman refereed the
Women's World Cup final when Ingrid Jonsson of Sweden took
charge.

Over the 26 matches, 99 goals were scored, and over 112,000
spectators watched the games, an average of 4,316 per match. Ann
Kristin Aarønes of Norway won the Golden Boot with six goals.
Norway also had a clean sweep of the best player awards when
Hege Riise won the Golden Ball for best player (she also scored
the first goal in the final), teammate Gro Espeseth came second,
and Aarønes third. [Side note: by hosting the 1995 women's event,
Sweden became the first country to host both the men's and the
women's World Cup after hosting the men's event in 1958.]

Profile: Birgit Prinz

Birgit Prinz was a forward and attacking midfielder for Germany. She began her senior career at FSV Frankfurt in 1993. During her time with them, she won two Bundesliga titles and two German Cups. She was the top scorer in the league in 1997 and 1998 and scored 45 goals in 57 appearances. She moved to local rivals 1. FFC Frankfurt in 1998, and during 13 seasons (with a two-year break at Carolina Courage in the U.S.), she scored over 200 goals, won the league's top-scorer award twice more, won six Bundesliga titles, eight German Cups, and the UEFA Women's Cup three times. Birgit also won German Female Footballer of the Year eight times and was FIFA World Player of the Year three times.

She made her debut for Germany, aged 16, in 1994, coming on as a sub and scoring the winning goal. She scored in the 1995 Euros final, aged 17, and in the 1995 World Cup, she became the youngest player to appear in a World Cup final (the record still stands). She won 5 Euros, 3 Olympic bronze medals, and 2 World Cups. She is Germany's most capped player (214) and top goalscorer (128), and the second all-time leading Women's World Cup goalscorer with 14 goals (behind Marta).

[Author's note: It was around the mid-1990s that I got my first proper opportunity to play football in a team. I was at university in Hertfordshire, and women's football was breaking into the consciousness of a few more people. I was thrilled to play. I remember strolling down to the astro pitch, a few minutes' walk from my student accommodation in the fading light of an October evening. I nervously met my fellow players, some freshers like me, some more experienced. We trained for a few weeks and then had our first home match. I don't remember much (I was running on pure adrenaline from fear and excitement), but I remember being put on the right wing. I remember racing up and down the pitch, but I'm not sure I got too many touches. We won convincingly, and I had played my first proper match. Finally. Sadly, it was also my last, thanks to a dodgy knee, which, many years later, it turned out I could have fixed relatively easily. It wasn't meant to be.]

Another first for women's football came in 1996 when the Atlanta Summer Olympics was the first to allow women to compete in the football event: another barrier broken and another opportunity to showcase the sport to a broader audience. Qualification came from the 1995 FIFA World Cup, and eight national teams (China, Japan, Brazil, Denmark, Germany, Norway, Sweden, and the U.S.) competed across two groups. Fighting for medals, China beat Brazil in semi-final one, and after extra time, the U.S. beat Norway in semi-final two. Norway won the bronze medal, and the final between the U.S. and China was played in front of 76,481 fans. In front of their home fans, the U.S. beat China 2-1 to take the first women's football Olympic gold medal.

In 1997, the Euros finally took on a full tournament format, and eight teams competed in the finals, which were co-hosted by Norway and Sweden. Germany and Italy met in the final, and Germany won their fourth UEFA European Championship title.

But the third FIFA World Cup in 1999 provided the watershed moment for women's football. The United States-hosted event was an iconic game-changer, thanks to the organising committee and the American players themselves. They wanted to create something that would change women's sport. They believed they could fill major stadiums. FIFA did not. FIFA wanted them to keep the event in smaller venues and wouldn't risk not being able to fill the larger stadiums. So, the organising committee took on the risk, and the matches were scheduled to be played in huge stadiums across the U.S. Feeling the sense of responsibility to fill the stadiums, the U.S. team went across the country promoting the tournament in schools, in towns, and anywhere they could, knocking on doors to make people aware of the event.

Thanks to the belief of the U.S. organising committee and the players, the tournament provided massive audiences, iconic moments, and new idols.

The event itself expanded to include 16 nations, the team of referees and match officials was female, and big names like McDonald's and Coca-Cola came on board to sponsor the spectacle. Four teams debuted at the tournament: Ghana, Mexico, North Korea, and Russia. They joined Australia, Brazil, Canada, China, Denmark, Germany, Italy, Japan, Nigeria, Norway, Sweden, and, of course, the U.S. in the biggest and best Women's World Cup so far. The U.S. beat Brazil in one semi-final, and China demolished holders Norway in the other. The scene was set for a final showdown. The final has gone down in football folklore as a stone-cold classic. The Rose Bowl stadium in Pasadena, California, is one of the biggest in the world, and on July 10th, 1999, it was packed with over 90,000 people. They had promoted women's football well beyond what had been achieved before, and there was one more match to show the world that women's football would no longer hide in the shadows. It was a heart-stopper.

The 90 minutes of normal time played out with a few attempts on goal, but nothing crossed the line. Extra time followed the same pattern, and the 90,000 crowd in the Rose Bowl Stadium were about to watch the first Women's World Cup Final penalty shootout. The first four penalty-takers found the back of the net as the tension built around the stadium and, indeed, the world. In the third round of penalties, Chinese player Liu Ying (sorry to have to name you here, Liu) had her penalty saved by the U.S. goalkeeper, Briana Scurry. There was later controversy around Scurry's save as she came off her line before the penalty was taken.

[Author's note: Having watched it again as research for this section of the book, there is no way that save should have counted. Briana is way off her line before Liu Ying has kicked the ball. Briana later admitted as much].

The following two takers for each team score, and it's now 4-4, with one more penalty to go. Brandi Chastain, the U.S. defender, has the stressful job of knowing she can win the World Cup with her spot kick. She buries it into the right-hand corner of the goal, beyond the goalkeeper. The U.S. team goes mad. And then Brandi Chastain provides an iconic, never-to-be-forgotten moment. She whips off her football shirt (jersey) and swirls it around her head before falling to her knees and double fist-pumping the air. It was an iconic moment forever preserved by the pitch-side photographers. Her black sports bra obviously got the media's attention, but it truly was an empowering moment for women's sport.

The U.S. lifted the World Cup trophy for the second time, and the tournament made history. Players became celebrities, appearing on talk shows, across the media, and in advertising campaigns, and the 99ers (as they became known) inspired future generations for years to come. The risk had been worth it. Average attendance figures were around 37,000 for each match, and the total attendance across the competition was nearly 1.2 million. Over 90,000 fans watched the final between the U.S. and China in the Rose Bowl in Pasadena, California. The U.S. television audience peaked at 40 million viewers (it was 15 years before the men's 2014 World Cup broke this record). Everything about it was huge. And it was a watershed moment.

Evolution Across the World

The British Isles

By the end of the decade, international football was unrecognisable from only a few years earlier. The next step was translating the major tournament excitement into building domestic leagues and year-round football.

Women's football was still mostly invisible in the UK during the early nineties, and girls still had to fight to play. About ten years after Issy Pollard's positive experience with a supportive head teacher at her primary school, Rachel Brown (now Rachel

Brown-Finnis) found herself in a similar position. After a couple of years of "unrelenting pressure and diving around on the playground," Rachel's PE teacher finally let her join the boys for PE, meaning she could play football on the grass. That's where it started, and she was soon on the school's B team before moving into their A team. Before long, she was playing in a Sunday League boys' team. By now, girls could play in a boys' team until they reached secondary school age but were then kicked out, mainly without a girls' team to go to. As I've discovered, the defining factor for girls who ended up playing football as women was determination. They didn't get to play if they didn't know what they wanted and went for it. Rachel went for it:

"It never dawned on me that when I went to secondary school, I couldn't play mixed football. I just thought it was football. I didn't think of girls' football or boys' football. I just thought it was playing football. So, just a simple consequence of going to secondary school: I couldn't play Sunday League, couldn't play at school, and I was like, oh my gosh, this can either be the end or what can I do? So, for a good year, there were no girls' teams to play for in my area. I ended up joining Accrington Stanley Ladies when I was in year eight. That fire, that determination, that resolve was always present. And I didn't really feel that anything was going to stop me. That wasn't through invincibility. It was just through sheer sort of will, determination, and wanting to play."

Rachel, who lived in Burnley, saw a Match magazine advert for a Bob Wilson goalkeeper camp in London. She persuaded her mum to let her go and spent Easter doing a five-day residential camp. It never occurred to her she would be the only girl, but her determination to play football kept her there. Luckily for women's football in England, it did. Her goalkeeper coach, Mick Payne, treated her like the boys and was positive and encouraging. Rachel returned the following year, and Mick encouraged her to find a better team. She trialled for Liverpool and spent the second half of the 1990s learning her trade with the Reds. But without Rachel's determination and the support of Mick Payne, things would have been different and were for most girls who wanted to play during this period.

There wasn't yet a pathway for girls in England, but the Women's Football Association (WFA) launched England's first national women's league for the 1991/92 season. Twenty-four clubs formed the league, made up of three divisions: National League Premier Division, Division 1 North, and Division 1 South. The top-tier Premier Division began with eight teams: Doncaster Belles, Red Star Southampton, Wimbledon, Knowsley United (later Liverpool), Maidstone Tigresses, Ipswich Town, Millwall Lionesses, and Notts Rangers.

It was during this period of the nineties that Doncaster Belles began dominating. They started by winning the first National League Premier Division title with a 100% record, winning all 14 league games in 1991/92. The league expanded to ten teams for the 1992/93 season, when Arsenal Ladies and Bronte Ladies were promoted as champions from the Southern and Northern Divisions, respectively. Issy Pollard played with Bronte at the time, before moving to Millwall Lionesses. As a 16-year-old, she moved away from her parents' home in the north east and moved to London to stay with a family who looked after her. Looking back on it now, she realises how big a step that was,

"Millwall Lionesses got me a job in a hotel on the Isle of Dogs. I didn't even think about it, but looking back now, as a 16-year-old, moving down to London, making my own way into Greenwich and the Greenwich Foot Tunnel. I must have been mature and independent!"

It was a different world for young footballers then.

In 1993, two years on from the new league, the WFA passed control to the FA. For the 20 years after the ban was lifted, the FA did little to help women's football grow, but now, as the official governing body, they set up a Women's Football Committee along with a full-time post for a Women's Football Coordinator. From the 1993/94 season, the WFA Cup also came under the control of the FA and became known as the Women's FA Cup. One hundred and forty teams entered the 1993/94 FA Cup, and Doncaster Belles beat Knowsley United in the final to complete a league and cup double. A year later, the top-flight division of the English league was rebranded as the FA Women's Premier League (FAWPL).

In the 1970s and 1980s, players began going to Italy to play semi-professional football. In the 1990s, players moved to Sweden for the same reasons. As a teenager, Issy Pollard was among the first to go to Sweden when she joined Betsele IF in 1994.

"We had a really good experience out there. Kind of semi-pro. You didn't get paid much, but you certainly didn't have to pay for anything. We all got accommodation, were well looked after, and had lots of training. That was amazing."

She later signed for Donny Belles, where she played with some of England's finest, Kaz Walker, Gill Coulthard, and Jackie Sherrard. In Issy's words, "pretty inspiring stuff". Issy described her time at Doncaster Belles as,

"Personally my greatest season because playing with them [sic] sort of players, you get found out if you can't play football. It was amazing."

During the decade, Arsenal began their dominance as Vic Akers continued to develop and add professionalism to all corners of the game, on and off the pitch. Throughout the decade, they won the league four times (three times in the top tier and once in tier two), four FA Cups, and five league cups.

In 1997, The FA set out strategic plans to grow football for girls and women from the grassroots through to the elite level. In 1998, 20 Centres of Excellence opened throughout the country. Instrumental in pushing this forward was Hope Powell, who had recently been appointed as the first full-time coach for England's national team. Hope oversaw the whole England setup from youth level to the senior team. Over the next 15 years, she made changes and fought battles that ultimately led to England's more recent successes. Hope Powell built the England women's setup from the ground up. She brought in physios, a medical officer, a sports scientist, and a goalkeeping coach for the first time. Together, they created a professional setup and changed how England's national team functioned.

Kelly Smith, legendary England striker, told the *The Athletic*,

"Hope put the foundations in for what it is now. She had to fight for everything — fight to have an office at Wembley, they didn't want to give her one. It is things like that people don't realise."

Until this point, everything about the England team set-up was completely amateur. Embarrassingly so.

Rachel Brown was called up to play for England in 1997 when she was 16. A couple of years later, she went to university in the United States and was lucky enough to be at the Rose Bowl in California for the final of the 1999 World Cup. She remembers sitting there, watching the game unfold, and thinking,

"These are international players. These are my peers. Every single one of those players is on the front pages of magazines and on chat shows, and everyone knows who they are. It was so far removed from what I was, as an England international. That was a real lightbulb moment where I was like, we are not respected in our country. We have no credibility; nobody sees us. We don't earn a penny from it. The standard's not good enough. We're not fit enough compared to, you know, Brandi Chastain whipping a shirt off with a six-pack. We were so far behind. So that lit a fire in me. And probably in Kelly, too [Kelly Smith, who was also in America at the time]. We wanted some of that, not for personal gain necessarily, but we wanted the credibility of the sport to be certainly better than it was. I really felt a deep sense of injustice as to how our sport was viewed in this country at the time, and I was like, I'm an England international; it's simply not good enough."

Rachel made it her mission to get the women's team seen. At every opportunity, she pointed out the current system's failings to people who could help. Everyone outside the immediate circle of the Lionesses assumed the setup must be great because it was English football. She told Prince William what it was really like. She contacted any new FA heads to get a line of communication within the FA and kept telling them how far behind the U.S. standards they were. She didn't do it for herself but for the England team to progress in the game.

Meanwhile, in Scotland, Sheila Begbie was appointed as the country's first Women's Football Coordinator in 1991. Her role was to develop girls' and women's football alongside the Scottish Football Association (SFA). The following year, Team Sport Scotland, the SFA, and the Scottish Women's Football Association (SWFA) began a joint initiative to plan the future of football for females in Scotland. At the end of the decade, the SFA also became involved in managing aspects of the game and took charge of the international team. They set up ten development centres, and in November 1999, the Scottish Women's Football League (SWFL) was formed, which created four divisions of football. In Wales, too, the organisation of the sport began to take shape. The Football Association Wales (FAW) Cup began in 1992. In 1993, the FAW took over control of women's football, including the running of the recently neglected international team. Wales played their first official friendly against Iceland in 1993 as a warm-up match to their 1995 Euros qualifiers. It was their only warm-up match, and with no infrastructure, training, or other friendlies to gain experience, they were understandably ill-prepared for the qualifying matches and lost them all. It was a new start for Wales but a tough one. There was no apparent progress in Northern Ireland, but the Republic of Ireland made some significant strides. In 1994, the Ladies Football Association of Ireland (LFAI), with support from Football Association Ireland (FAI), began a development programme for girls and introduced under-16 and under-20s international teams to form a pathway to the senior national team.

Europe

As other teams became more competitive, Italy generally found it more challenging to qualify for major tournaments. They were, however, runners-up to Germany at the 1997 Euros. They were still at the forefront of organisational change, though. At the start of the decade, Marina Sbardella was made president of their Women's Football Committee, responsible for running the women's section under the Italian governing body. By the end of the decade, Carolina Morace had become the first woman to coach a professional men's team when she took over Viterbese, who were in the Italian Serie C1 league.

Germany dominated the Euros through the 1990s, but their domestic football was only just starting. In 1990, a German Democratic Republic (East Germany) league began, and in

West Germany, the German Football Association created the semi-professional Frauen-Bundesliga. It began with north and south divisions, which merged to mirror the men's league in 1997.

Sweden and Norway provided the most competition to Germany in international football. Since gender stereotyping is widely discouraged in these countries, the development of their teams was supported much sooner than in other countries. With their league first established in 1971, the country's investment in time and infrastructure helped develop the game more quickly than most other countries. In 1990, while many nations were still working out infrastructure and setting up national teams, Sweden played their 100th international match. The Project Group Women's Football was set up in 1994 to continue to develop football and female leaders within the sport. In 1995, Ingrid Jonsson became the first woman to referee in a FIFA final when she was assistant referee at the Women's 1991 World Cup. Sweden was miles ahead of most other countries when it came to opportunities for women and girls in football. Norway promoted women in sport too, and their female referee, Bente Skogvang, officiated at Sweden's 1995 World Cup and the first women's Olympic final in 1996. Norway became World Champions in 1995 when they beat Germany in the World Cup final. Denmark continued to reach the latter stages of competitions throughout the nineties but struggled to drive the game forward in the same way as their neighbours.

Rest of the World

The 1999 World Cup will always define women's football in the 1990s. The U.S. team will always be remembered as iconic trailblazers. They took the game to a new level. In preparation for the 1991 World Cup, the USWNT played exhibition matches in Europe. The players quit their jobs to train full-time, even though they had hardly any financial compensation for playing. Their drive, ambition, and professionalism helped them win the first World Cup trophy. The team that had only formed six years earlier smashed Chinese Taipei 7-0 *en route* to the trophy when Michelle Akers scored five goals in the first 50 minutes of the match. A hat-trick from Carin Jennings helped them beat Germany in the semi-final; their attacking drive was virtually impossible to stop. Although they were now World Champions, when the team arrived home, only a few people were there to greet them. Women's football still had a way to go.

Despite the historic 1991 victory, the U.S. Soccer resources, and attention were soon directed towards the men's qualification campaign for their home World Cup in 1994. Consequently, the Women's World Champions only played twice in 1992. In 1994, with their title to defend at the 1995 World Cup, they began their preparations. With few international opportunities nearby, the team went to the inaugural Algarve Cup in Portugal and competed against some of the best teams in Europe. Their conditions at home improved when, in 1995, a training and treatment facility was built to help them prepare effectively for the defence of their world title. But there was no fairy tale this time, and the team finished third. It was an amazing decade for the USWNT, though.

On home soil, they won both the first Olympic gold and the World Cup. But although the U.S. had an incredible national team that had developed from a strong college system, they didn't have a professional women's league. In 1995, the semi-professional W-League began and continued even after a group split away to form the Women's Premier Soccer League (WPSL) in 1998 (also an amateur/semi-professional league). But by the end of the 1990s, there was no hint of a fully professional league.

Unfortunately for Canada, the injection of resources into the U.S. team meant it was difficult for them to compete for the one regional qualifying spot for the 1991 World Cup. Once the U.S. had claimed the spot, the Canadian national programme stalled, and the team didn't play an international for the next two years. Despite the setback, they qualified for the 1995 World Cup when two spots were allocated to the federation.

Their first World Cup game was against England, and although they lost 3-2, a late fightback meant they scored their first World Cup goals, the first by Helen Stoumbos and the second by Geri Donelly. They drew their next game against Nigeria to win their first championship point.

Brazil had a rapid rise to the top of international football after finishing the previous decade as bronze medallists at the World Cup test event in 1988. In 1991, they won the first Copa América Femenina (the women's version of the South American

Profile: Mia Hamm

You can't talk about the USWNT in the 1990s without mentioning Mia Hamm, possibly the biggest name in women's football. Born in 1972, Mia helped the U.S. win two Olympic gold medals and two World Cups. At 15, she became the youngest player in the U.S. team and was only 19 when they won the inaugural FIFA World Cup in China in 1991. She played in three Olympic tournaments, including the first in Atlanta in 1996, and won gold at both the 1996 and 2004 Games. Her career spanned three decades, from 1987 to 2004. Across the three Olympics and four World Cups she attended, she played 42 matches and scored 14 goals. Her total international tally is 276 caps, with 158 goals and 144 assists. Her college team, the North Carolina Tar Heels, won four NCAA championships: helped by Mia's 103 goals in 95 games between 1989 and 1993. Mia was FIFA World Player of the Year in 2001 and 2002, and in 2004, Pelé chose her as one of FIFA's 125 greatest living players. Named U.S. Soccer Female Athlete of the Year five years in a row, she has been inducted into the National Soccer Hall of Fame and was the first woman to be inducted into the World Football Hall of Fame. She's kind of a big deal in football. She now co-owns Angel City FC and remains very much involved in women's football.

Championships, Copa América) to qualify for the first FIFA World Cup. The Copa América Femenina, organised by the South American Football Confederation, came about 75 years after the men's version but was a welcome promotion for women's football in the region. Brazil beat Chile and Venezuela to represent South America at the World Cup but crashed out of the FIFA competition early. They did score their first World Cup goal, courtesy of Elane, though. Similarly, in the 1995 World Cup, Brazil struggled against the teams that had been established for longer. But the gap had narrowed by 1999, and they finished third. Perhaps the growth in women's football across Brazil during the decade is best demonstrated by these statistics, though: in 1991, there were 20 women's clubs across the country; in 1995, there were 420 clubs.

New Zealand debuted at the 1991 FIFA World Cup after they beat Australia to be the Oceania confederation's representative. But they had to wait a while before they qualified again (until Australia changed confederation, actually) as Australia became the dominant Oceania team. For New Zealand, the women's domestic game grew hugely through the nineties, when many new clubs formed, but it was Australia that grew on the world stage. After winning the 1994 Oceania Cup, Australia qualified for their first World Cup in 1995 and became known as the "Matildas" for the first time. Since then, Australia has qualified for every FIFA World Cup. The domestic game in Australia developed with a national league, the Ansett Australia Summer Series, which began in 1996.

As the club football competition became more established in China, so did their national team. Throughout the 1990s, China won all five editions of the Women's Asian Cup, plus the Asian Games in 1990 and 1994. They dominated the game in Asia and hosted the first FIFA Women's World Cup. The event drew in 510,000 spectators over the tournament, and although China lost in the quarter-finals, tens of thousands of people came out to watch them and were exposed to women's football for the first time. They came fourth in the 1995 World Cup and were keen to medal in the 1996 Olympics. So, they undertook intense preparations with the full support of their Football Association. They entered 18 international competitions and spent four months in training camps in the United States in preparation. Their dedication paid off when they won the silver medal. In 1997, the Chinese Women's Super League was founded on the back of the national team's success.

African football boomed, too. In Nigeria, Princess Jegede had financed their first national tournament, and the same year, the Nigeria Women's Premier League (now known as the NWFL Premiership) formed. The most significant advancement came in 1991 when the first African Women's Championship began. Now known as the Women's Africa Cup of Nations, the biennial championship is organised by the Confederation of African Football and provides regular competition for African nations and a qualification route to the World Cup. Nigeria — nicknamed the Super Falcons — won the first title by beating Ghana, which qualified them for the World Cup in 1991. In 1999, Nigeria recorded their best World Cup result (at the time of writing) when they reached the quarter-finals. They lost against Brazil via a golden goal in extra time, but the two teams made history by being the first to contest a Women's World Cup match decided by the controversial golden goal.

[Side note: The golden goal — for a period in the 1990s and 2000s, knockout games were decided by a "golden goal". If the teams were level at the end of normal time, the game went into extra time. The game was played for a further 30 additional minutes (2 halves of 15 minutes) but was stopped as soon as a goal was scored: the "golden goal". It was hoped this would lead to more attacking and exciting football in extra time, but it is now largely considered a failed experiment. The golden goal was soon dropped.]

Ghana also qualified for the 1999 World Cup as African football developed. Teams formed in Kenya in the 1980s and in 1993, the Kenya Women's Football Federation was started by two local women. The federation sponsored a national team that competed until 1996 when the male-controlled Kenya Football Federation took over the running and created a subcommittee for the women's team. As other countries across the world found, the men's federation did little, if anything, to progress the women's team. Regardless of the support, football fever spread, and in 1993, the South African women's team played its first international match against Eswatini (formerly Swaziland). By 1997, there were around 67,000 women playing in South Africa. The Senegalese Football Federation set up their first Women's Championship in 1992, but the event was sporadically held through the decade.

Across the world, the 1990s were about trying to break through footballing glass ceilings. The first FIFA World Cup was the first sign this was possible. Germany and Sweden proved how backing from federations helped propel teams to the top, and this inspired England to want the same. English football made significant progress for female footballers during the decade, driven by Hope Powell and her team, and the opening of Centres of Excellence paved the way for greater success. Italy's Carolina Morace made history by becoming the first woman to coach a men's team, and the U.S. National Women's Team fought to make sure their home

World Cup was the biggest and best the world had seen, making themselves global icons along the way. The 99ers, including Mia Hamm, Michelle Akers, Julie Foudy, and Brandi Chastain, are still global icons 25 years later.

11

The 2000s: New Growth

England, the U.S. and a Game Changing Film

It felt like everything would change in women's football after
the 1999 World Cup. The U.S. had hosted a record-breaking
tournament, produced superstars, and set the football world
alight. Vast numbers of people now knew that not only did women
play football, but they played it to a high level. The game had
changed.

Or had it? A pattern emerged. People got excited about major
tournaments, supported their countries, went to the games,
watched on TV, and got caught up in the excitement of
tournament football. But between the major tournaments,
interest waned, mostly because of the lack of strong (or any)
leagues. Between the major tournaments, the sport was hardly
shown. In England, the Women's FA Cup Final was still the only
domestic game broadcast each year, so there was no real visibility
outside of international events. Despite the progress across the
world, women's football was, at best, a semi-professional sport

and then only in a handful of countries. Amateur players needed part-time jobs, and this limited their time to train. In England, this led to constant criticism that women's football was of poor quality compared to men's (well, yes, elite men didn't have to treat football like a hobby), so it wasn't worth promoting. Without promotion or visibility in the media, league matches stayed the domain of hardcore fans only. Fortunately, England still had Hope. Hope Powell, that is.

Germany, Italy, Sweden, Norway, Denmark, and the U.S. were the only countries that had invested time and money into leagues at this point. Italy, Sweden, Denmark, and Germany had semi-professional leagues with the odd fully professional team, but England, the founders of association football, had no professional clubs. England's men's Premier League was considered the biggest and best in the world, so if England weren't bothered about women's football, how serious could it be? Like it or not, England has a major influence on world football. But this began to change at the start of the new millennium when Fulham Ladies, with a huge cash injection, became England's first professional club. The game was slowly growing in England thanks to Hope Powell's persistence and hard work to raise both the standards and profile of women's football. This chapter's thread will follow the game's development in England but will still be within the context of world football. Germany, the Nordic countries, Italy, and the U.S. had shown what was possible. Could England respond?

In 2001, the English FA increased the number of Centres of Excellence to fifty to provide more top-class coaching. These

Centres provided a pathway from grassroots football in towns and villages to potentially playing the sport at the top level. Alongside the Centres of Excellence, Hope Powell began the first scholarship programme, which allowed nineteen players to receive fully funded scholarships to attend the Loughborough Player Development Centre. This meant they could continue their education whilst also being coached by top coaches. Since most clubs were still part-time, the scholarships allowed players such as Ellen White, Jill Scott, and Karen Carney to study beyond GCSEs whilst also training. The FA funded the places with an eye on developing the national setup so they could challenge for the 2007 World Cup.

The development pathway made it easier for players to develop once they'd been spotted by the FA, but what was being done to encourage girls into football at the grassroots level? Nothing really. And then along came a movie.

Before 2002, in many countries, girls playing football was still considered odd. Few girls played in England, and many probably thought they were the only girl who did. But that changed in 2002 thanks to the cultural touchpoint movie, "Bend It Like Beckham". Created and directed by Gurinder Chadha, it became a cult classic for an entire generation of girls and women across the world, and it was particularly important for Asian females. Within a story about girls in football, the film tackled major cultural issues, including racism, sexism, homophobia, and the complexities of the life of an Asian girl navigating the modern world amongst her traditional upbringing. This was the first time Asian girls had seen themselves represented in such a way on screen. It changed football across the world and across cultures.

When I asked Gurinder Chadha how the film was received amongst Asian communities, she told me,

"It's a die-hard favourite. It was able to really reflect the multiplicity of our lives within the community. It was the first film for lots of women that really spoke to the different sides of themselves, and it was positive, and the girl ends up getting everything. I'm constantly getting people saying to me, your film inspired my daughter to take up football. And in India when the film came out, there were a few leagues set up, the Bend It Like Beckham leagues, where women set up their own leagues and started playing."

What an impact.

If you're not familiar with it (or it's been a while), the film was based around British Indian girl Jesminder (Jess), who loved football but was hampered both by being a girl and being part of a traditional Indian family and the expectations that came along with that. She met white British girl, Jules, who after seeing Jess' skills on the ball invited her to join a local team. Jesminder's parents forbid her. Jess, of course, joined the team anyway and played behind her family's back.

"Bend It Like Beckham" is funny, but it's also a tale of friendship, of love, of adversity, and ultimately of how a girl's love for football wins out. It spoke to a generation. It raised the profile of the game, particularly among Asian girls who now saw themselves represented for the first time as footballers. The film made it acceptable for girls to play, and the number of players soared as millions had their first taste of women's football. It didn't just bring Asian girls into the game, as Gurinder told me,

"And it's not just Indian women, the England team and the U.S. team have all gone on record [to say] most of the players only started [playing] after watching Bend It Like Beckham."

It dispelled the myth that girls can't play and made it visible to generations of women and girls. If you haven't seen it, I urge you to seek it out. If you saw it in 2002, go and watch it again. It may be even more emotional considering where football is now.

Gurinder Chadha is a visionary and trailblazer for women playing football. When she first approached people about the film, they thought women playing football was "a total joke". When I asked how she felt about that now, she said she felt "vindicated".

"People laughed at it, and not only was that a joke but also that an Indian girl being able to bend the ball was seen as really ludicrous and so people didn't take it seriously. If you'd have said to me back then that it was going to be on TV, national TV, the women's game, everyone would have said I was mad, but now it being part of mainstream sports fixtures on TV globally is incredible. Vindication is the right word."

It took Gurinder three years to get it made because no one believed in it. The film was a smash hit, bringing in nearly £60 million from the Box Office. Definitely vindicated.

[Author note: On a personal note, this film made me feel seen. Although I was being called a "tomboy" 15 years earlier than the setting of the film, in a part of the country where there were no teams with girls, it completely resonated. Jesminder's circumstances may have been a million miles away from mine, but the feelings about football were the same. Rather than David Beckham posters on the wall, I had posters of previous Manchester United legends, Bryan Robson, Mark Hughes, and Norman Whiteside. But the feelings about wanting to play football were the same. Unfortunately, social attitudes didn't change much in the intervening years.]

The same year as the film, the FA announced that football was now the most played team sport by women and girls in England. The FA's recent strategic plan had set 2005 as the target for achieving this figure, but they reached it three years early. I think this shows the demand was always there, but the visibility wasn't. The increasingly televised World Cups and Bend it Like Beckham helped girls see the possibilities.

Within Bend It Like Beckham, one storyline sees the girls pursue a football scholarship in the U.S. At the time, in England, there was only one professional team, which meant for most footballers, training was part-time, and players needed jobs. The reality, even at successful teams like Arsenal, was that playing football cost them money as they needed to buy kit and pay for travel, as well as get time off work (you'll hear it referred to as "pay to play"). The alternative to struggling in England was to get a scholarship to college in the United States to play.

Many top-name British players did just that and left England behind to get a traditional education alongside a top-level football education. Kelly Smith — one of England's greatest ever players — won the 1996/97 Women's Premier League title with Arsenal and then jetted across to New Jersey to play college football. Alex Scott, Rachel Brown-Finnis, and more recently, Rachel Daly, Lotte Wubben-Moy, and Alessia Russo all played football in the U.S. before returning home to England.

One of, if not the most important step within English football, was the introduction of central contracts for players. Started by Hope Powell in 2009, the FA gave 17 players contracts of £16,000 a year. This enabled them to train full-time, which meant England's chances of success at future international tournaments could be improved. Players no longer had the distraction of having to work another job and could focus solely on their football. For the first time, they were professional footballers. The agreement came a few months before the 2009 Euros finals, and the first players to benefit were Rachel Brown (now Rachel Brown- Finnis), Siobhan Chamberlain, Carly Telford, Casey Stoney, Faye White, Rachel Unitt, Steph Houghton, Emily Westwood, Katie Chapman, Jill Scott, Laura Bassett, Rachel Williams, Rachel Yankey, Sue Smith, Jody Handley, Lindsay Johnson, and Corrine Yorston. It quickly became clear that investment works, and the Lionesses picked up their first international trophy in decades when they won the 2009 Cyprus Cup.

In the U.S., despite the successes on the pitch, the work the players did to promote the game, and the solid amateur leagues, it had been difficult to translate international success into a professional league. With all that Title IX had brought, their college system was the best in the world and turned out world-class footballers constantly. But once players graduated, there was no way to earn a living from football in their home country. A professional league was planned before the 1999 success but had been delayed when U.S. Soccer got twitchy (they did the same when setting up the men's professional Major League Soccer, MLS, a few years previously). Finally, in 2000, U.S. Soccer agreed to start a women's pro football (soccer) league. They were in a strong position, with solid investment and a plan. In April 2001, the Women's United Soccer Association (WUSA), the first fully professional league in the world, began. With the backing of U.S. Soccer and investment from sponsors, eight teams began the first women's professional league: Atlanta Beat, Bay Area CyberRays, Boston Breakers, Carolina Tempest, New York Power, Philadelphia Charge, San Diego Spirit, and Washington Freedom (can we just take a minute to appreciate the cool names the U.S. teams have?). Almost all the 1999 World Cup stars, along with a good mix of big international stars, including Sun Wen of China and Birgit Prinz of Germany, had signed up for the new domestic league. Having the stars from recent World Cups could really help boost the first professional league's appeal and bring in the audience. All looked good.

With enough sponsors, they hoped to get the league off the ground and bring in enough spectators to make it sustainable, but although they got some major sponsors, they struggled to find enough who would back the project. Attendances and viewing figures dropped off in the second season, and after three seasons,

Profile: Kelly Smith

Kelly Smith was a formidable striker, breaking records both in England and the U.S. She began her senior career at Wembley Ladies before moving to Arsenal for a season in 1996, helping them win the Premier League title. It also helped her a place at Seton Hall Pirates in the U.S. She won the Big East Offensive Player of the Year and Newcomer of the Year awards in the same season, the first athlete to do so. Whilst there, she scored 76 goals in 51 appearances. Kelly played for several teams in the U.S. because "women's football in England is a joke". In 2005, Kelly moved back to Arsenal and was a key part of the 2006/07 quadruple-winning squad that won the league, the FA Cup, the League Cup, and the UEFA Women's Cup (now the Champions League). Kelly scored 30 goals in 34 games. She continued to criss-cross the Atlantic, playing for Arsenal and the Boston Breakers.

Her England debut came in November 1995, a few days before she turned 17. In her second match, she scored her first goal and didn't stop. In 117 internationals, she scored 46 goals. She competed in three Euros and two World Cups. In 2010, she became England's all-time top goal scorer. Her tally of 46 goals has now been overtaken by Ellen White's 52. In 2008, Kelly Smith was awarded an MBE.

the league folded. The teams continued to play exhibition matches for a while but were forced to fold soon after. It was a devastating time for U.S. women footballers, who had to completely rethink their careers. It also sent out the message that women's football didn't have a fan base that would support league football. The players went back to play amateur or semi-professional football. A few years passed without a professional league in the U.S. until the Women's Professional Soccer League (WPSL) began in 2007. The story was like last time, though, and a sustainable league remained out of reach, even for the best players in the world. The league folded after three seasons. With a popular and influential college competition and a successful national team, the U.S. still couldn't make a professional league stick. The support for the women's league wasn't what it could have been and it was hugely disappointing for the players, who fought so hard to get equality. As yet, nowhere could offer anything more than semi-professional football to women.

[Side note: for some context, in England, the fourth division of men's football in the country in the early 2000s was earning an average salary of about £28,000 per year with attendances of about 4,000 spectators. Although there are other factors to consider, it doesn't seem unreasonable that a professional league was attainable for women at this time].

Across Scotland, there was significant progress, too. In 2001, Ross County became the first team in Scotland to employ female apprentice footballers, making them professional players. They were funded by the Scottish FA (SFA), and soon, other teams followed, and new development centres opened. In 2002, there was a major milestone for league football when the then Premier Division broke away to form the Scottish Women's Premier League (SWPL). By separating the top teams, they aimed to highlight the best of the game, leading to more attention from the media and influential decision-makers. It was a marker in the sand in Scotland. Twelve teams founded the first SWPL: Ayr United, Cove Rangers, Dundee, Giulianos, Glasgow City FC,

Hamilton Academical, Hibernian, Inver-Ross, FC Kilmarnock, Lossiemouth, Raith Rovers, and Shettleson.

Profile: Hope Powell

Born in 1966, Hope made headlines, aged 11, the FA banned her from playing for her school team (because of the age rules then). She began playing for Millwall Lionesses, before moving to Friends of Fulham a decade later. She played in the 1989 FA Cup final whilst there, scoring twice (they still lost). Hope moved back to Millwall Lionesses and became their all-time top goalscorer. She won the 1991 FA Cup with them, but soon after, the team broke up. Hope, alongside Brenda Sempare, formed Bromley Borough (later part of Croydon). Hope captained Croydon to a league and cup double in 1995/96.

She debuted for England in 1983, aged 16, and was part of the 1984 Euros. She was vice-captain for the 1995 World Cup, and during her 66 caps, she scored 35 goals. In 1998, she became the first full-time England women's coach. In 2003, she became the first woman to earn a UEFA Pro Licence — the highest coaching qualification. Hope led the Lionesses to four Euros and to World Cup quarter-finals in 2007 and 2011. She oversaw the England setup, from youth to senior. It's no exaggeration to say Hope Powell paved the way for future success. She won two Cyprus Cups and led England to the 2009 Euros final. In 2012, she was awarded a CBE for her contribution to women's football, and she was inducted into English Football's Hall of Fame in 2003.

The remaining 30 teams in the league made up three divisions of the Scottish Women's Football League (SWFL). Appropriately, Kilmarnock won the first championship in 2002/2003, the team that had formerly been known as Stewarton Thistle.

The same year, the Scottish national team broke into the Top 20 teams in Europe for the first time. By the end of the decade, the Scottish FA had taken over running women's football from Scottish Women's Football Limited and brought it under the same umbrella as men's football. Glasgow City showed their class and became the first Scottish club to reach the last 16 of the Women's Champions League in 2008/09. Within the next decade, the team reached the quarter-finals twice. In 2009, the league moved from a winter one to a summer one, which ran from March to November. This was the opposite way around to the English league, but there were methods in the madness. Running a summer league meant there were fewer postponements for unplayable pitches, and more fans came out to watch the games. In the 11 seasons of summer football, Glasgow City won all the titles, so it suited them. During this time, they also won several domestic trebles.

There was positive progress in Wales, and by the end of the noughties, the Welsh Premier Women's Football League had been set up. Eight clubs formed the first Premier League (Aberystwyth Town Ladies, Caernarfon Town, Llanidloes, Moanorbier, Newcastle Emlyn, Swansea City, Cardiff Met, and Wrexham). The league is now known as the Adran Premier (the Premier Division) after a conscious decision was taken in 2021 to drop the "women's" label to encourage parity with the men's equivalent league. The league isn't yet professional.

Europe

Although the Division 1 Féminine (D1F) in France was established
in 1975, it still wasn't professional by the start of the new
millennium. But then the club side Olympique Lyonnais burst
into the conversation and changed the course of football in France.
FC Lyon formed in 1970, but in 2004 the men's club, Olympique
Lyonnais, took over the running of the team and incorporated it
into their club and brand. The club fully embraced the women's
team and gave them unprecedented support. Olympique Lyonnais
Féminin was born, and they rapidly became one of the best
club sides in the world. Lyon, as they're known, won their first
league title in 2007 and then extended that league title into a
14-year league winning streak (before coming second in 2020/21).
They have boasted many of the world's best players, including
Hope Solo, Megan Rapinoe, Alex Morgan, Nikita Parris, Alex
Greenwood, and Lucy Bronze, and at the time of writing, have
won 30 domestic trophies (league and cup) and eight Champions
League titles. They undoubtedly helped raise the standard of
football in France and drive the D1F towards professionalism. By
the end of the decade, some players in some teams were signing
professional contracts.

There was a similar story in Spain. The first Barcelona women's
team was founded in 1970, and although they weren't officially
part of the men's club then, they did receive some support from
them. When the first national women's league was set up in
Spain in 1988, Barcelona was a founding member. It was only
in 2002 that the team became known as Club Femení Barcelona

and officially became part of FC Barcelona, though. At this point, the team was in the Spanish second division (the lowest tier at the time). They competed in the playoffs in 2002 and 2003, but it wasn't until 2004 that they were promoted to the Superliga Feminina (Spain's top division, now known as Liga F). Despite attracting some top-class players, they could not keep their place in the top league and were relegated back to the second tier at the end of the 2006/07 season. This prompted concerns about the team's future. In 2008, they returned to the Superliga, and their golden era began. In 2009, they won the Catalan Cup, and in 2011/12, they won the league for the first time.

Perhaps the biggest sign that club football had taken hold in Europe was the introduction of the UEFA Women's Cup in 2001, later known as the Women's Champions League. In its first season, the tournament welcomed 33 teams, and the last two standing were Umeå of Sweden and FFC Frankfurt of Germany. Frankfurt won the final in May 2002. The competition grew, and two years after the first, 40 teams entered; although Frankfurt and Umeå dominated the event in the early years. In 2006/07, England got their first (and so far, only) Women's Champions League winning team when Arsenal, having the season of their lives, beat Umeå over two closely fought final legs. They became the first team outside of Germany or Scandinavia to win. Arsenal won a quadruple that season. Lyon and Barcelona have dominated in more recent years. Attendances have grown over the years, and the Nou Camp in Barcelona holds the record when, in 2021/22, a whopping 91,648 people watched their semi-final against Wolfsburg. The next highest attendance was also at the

Nou Camp for a Champions League quarter-final against Real
Madrid, where 91,553 watched. And no one watches women's
sports. Pfft.

Rest of the World

As the World Cup gained popularity, countries began creating
stronger domestic competitions. In Brazil in 2007, the Copa do
Brasil de Futebol Feminino (Brazil Women's Cup) — equivalent
to the men's Copa de Brasil — was set up by the Brazilian
Football Confederation and the Ministry of Sport. As part of
the setup, the confederation made a separate women's refereeing
staff for the competition. As domestic competition grew, so did
the strength of the national side and Brazil were runners-up
at both the 2007 World Cup and the 2008 Olympics. At the
end of the decade, the South American Football Confederation
(CONMEBOL) set up the Libertadores Feminina annual
international club competition for teams in South America
(equivalent to the men's competition). In 2019, the competition
stipulated that men's teams could only be a part of it if
they had a women's team — a change made to strengthen
women's football. Over the course of the competition, Brazil's
Corinthians have so far been the most successful.

In 2002, New Zealand's week-long National Women's
Tournament held once a year, was developed into a weekly league
format, meaning domestic teams could play competitive games
every week. In Australia, the Ansett Summer Series of state
teams gradually turned into the National Women's Soccer League

club league, and in 2008, Australia's top club competition, the W-League, was launched.

To make football sustainable and competitive, leagues had to develop. With time, the excitement that built around the Euros, Olympics, and the World Cup would filter across to weekly audiences for club football. With more structure and semi-professional leagues, plus the odd fully professional club, strength in national teams could grow, and international competitions would become more competitive. International success boosts excitement for league football, quality gets better, and the cycle continues as domestic and international football build together. And excitement for major tournaments certainly increased throughout the noughties.

Major Tournaments

For England, the 2005 Euros was the first time they had hosted a major international women's football event. It finally demonstrated commitment to women's football and provided a springboard for later success. It's no coincidence that the countries who had hosted Euros competitions (Norway, Denmark, Sweden, Germany, and Italy) had been the most successful. In line with the English FA's strategic plan to grow the game, hosting the 2005 Euros was an opportunity to invest and drive the game forward. And in the UK, when we put our minds to it, we're pretty good at organising things and very good at coming out to support them. The event drew record crowds: both in stadiums and via TV audiences. Over 29,000 people went to the City of Manchester

Stadium to watch England's opening match against Finland —
a record crowd at the time for a match in Europe and a figure
that dwarfed the 18,000-odd spectators who watched the final
in Germany four years previously. The spectators experienced a
thriller when Finland equalised in the 88th minute, only to see
Karen Carney score the winner for England in stoppage time.
Unfortunately, from a football point of view, this was the highlight
of England's tournament as they lost both remaining group games
against tough Danish and Swedish sides. Attendance figures were
excellent, England's results, not so much. Germany beat Norway
in the final to win their fourth successive title (sixth overall) in
front of a then-record crowd for a final of 21,105.

Despite the disappointing on-field display, the tournament was
a success for football in England. Eurosport screened every game
live, and the BBC showed England's group games and the final.
Throughout the tournament's 15 matches, 117,384 spectators
attended games, averaging 7,894 per match. The TV audience
for England's game against Sweden was over 3.5 million, which
represented about 20% of the total available English audience.
After the event, UEFA CEO Lars-Christer Olsson said, "The fact
we were successful in the homeland of football will also have
positive effects in all other countries around Europe. I'm sure we
will move women's football to another level." This wasn't just
a win for women's football in England; its ripple effects were
felt throughout Europe. Where once the banning of football in
England spread across the world, now the excitement for it did.

Profile: Abby Wambach

Abby Wambach was one of the world's greats. During her international career, she played 255 times for the USWNT and scored an incredible 184 goals. She also set records at the University of Florida with 96 goals, 49 assists, and 10 hat-tricks.

Abby's international career began in 2001 before even having a senior club team. In 2002, she joined Washington Freedom. She was named U.S. Soccer's Female Athlete of the Year in 2003, 2004, 2007, 2010, 2011, and 2013. In 2004, she scored 31 goals and recorded 13 assists in 30 matches for the USWNT. In the 2004 Olympics final, Abby scored a header in the 112th minute to secure the gold medal. She broke her leg just before the 2008 Olympics, but at London 2012, she scored in every game except the final (five goals). But Abby didn't win a World Cup in any of her first three competitions. The 2015 World Cup was now or never for the veteran. She captained the team in the first few games and came off the bench in later matches as the new generation of players took over. By the end of the tournament, Abby Wambach had added another World Cup goal and lifted the World Cup trophy for the first time.

Abby was voted FIFA World Player of the Year in 2012 and was named one of the world's most influential people in 2015.

The genie was out of the bottle. With increased visibility, the game drew more interest from women and girls who wanted to play and watch. If you can see it, you can be it. Teams other than Germany and the Scandinavian countries started showing the fruits of investment, and England was a good example.

Although not performing as well as hoped at their home Euros in 2005, the Lionesses ended the noughties with a roar when they performed much better at the 2009 Euros. They knocked out

hosts Finland in the quarter-finals and then squeaked past The
Netherlands in the semi-finals (with a Jill Scott winner towards
the end of extra time). The Lionesses reached the Euros final
for only the second time in their history — the first time was
way back at the first UEFA event in 1984. It was another pivotal
moment in the sport in England and football fever hit the nation.
Unfortunately, they had to face perennial winners Germany in
the trophy match. Nearly 16,000 people watched the final in
Helsinki, but it wasn't a great contest as Germany easily won
6-2. It was bitterly disappointing for England, but getting to
that final proved they had built the foundations. They'd spent
decades in the football wilderness because of a lack of resources,
facilities, and structure. However, reaching the final of a European
Championship to face the world's best was a sign that what
Hope Powell and the FA were doing was working. Finishing as
runners-up was disappointing, but it gave England something to
build on, and the next generation of England stars showed their
promise when the young Lionesses lifted the under-19s Euros
trophy in Belarus. The team included future stars Lucy Bronze,
Jordan Nobbs, and Toni Duggan.

Olympic football wasn't an event England competed in (because
there was no Great Britain football team), but it was fiercely
contested by the rest of the world. As defending champions from
1996, the U.S. hoped they'd win another gold medal at the Sydney
Olympics in 2000. In the end, they were defeated in the final by
an extra-time golden goal scored by Norway's Dagny Mellgren.
In Athens in 2004, the U.S. were again involved in a thrilling
gold medal match that went to extra time. The score was one-all

at full-time, but Abby Wambach scored the winner in the 112th minute to secure a second gold for the USWNT. Brazil won the silver medal in the first of Marta's six Olympic Games, and Germany won bronze. In Beijing in 2008, the Olympic football competition expanded to 12 teams. Brazil, Germany, Japan, and the U.S. reached the semi-finals, and with Marta and Cristiane firing on all cylinders, Brazil cruised past Germany with a 4-1 win. There were plenty of goals in the other semi-final, too, as the U.S. beat Japan 4-2. It was all set up for an exciting showdown between the U.S. and Brazil, but after the high-scoring semi-finals, the gold medal match was a bit of an anti-climax with a single goal in extra time, winning another gold for the U.S. Germany won the bronze medal. Attendance figures were much higher than the previous Olympics, averaging 28,462 per match. The highest attendance was for a group match between hosts China and Canada when 52,600 people watched the teams draw. 51,612 people watched the gold medal match.

The main event was, of course, the World Cup. In 2003, it was switched from being hosted by China to the U.S. at the last minute because of the SARS outbreak in China. Three teams made their World Cup debut in 2003: Argentina, France, and South Korea, but England failed to qualify (useful to note in the context of their development). Of the 16 teams who began the tournament, the U.S., Germany, Sweden, and Canada reached the semi-finals. Germany caused a major upset when they beat the U.S. because, despite Germany's dominance in Europe, this was only the second loss the U.S. had suffered at a World Cup. Germany won their first Women's World Cup with a golden goal in extra time. Although smaller than the carefully organised 1999 event, the average match attendance was still 21,240, which, considering the late change in the host country, was very positive.

As China could not host the 2003 World Cup, they were automatically granted the 2007 competition to host. Sixteen teams from six confederations once more competed, and England qualified for only their second-ever FIFA World Cup appearance (the last time was way back in 1995). As Rachel Brown-Finnis told me, it might have been a long time coming, but it was huge for the players.

"I was 27 when we went to our first World Cup. For current people either watching the Lionesses or even the current Lionesses [themselves], that's 10 years of an England career before I got to a World Cup. That just wouldn't happen again. And that's great, that's where we are now, which is fantastic. That was a monumental moment, something that all of us who actually achieved it, to get over that final hurdle meant a huge amount, and it opened the door to bigger and better conversations with the FA, more resources, and progress. And that's what we wanted."

However, England's tournament draw wasn't kind, as they were grouped with Germany and Japan. Unexpectedly, England's Lionesses played out a scoreless draw against holders Germany in front of 27,000 people in Shanghai, which helped them qualify for the quarter-finals. It clearly wasn't to be England's tournament, though, because they met the U.S. in the quarter-finals. They lost 3-0. Germany, Norway, and Brazil qualified for the semi-finals alongside the United States. Germany beat Norway in their semi-final, but there was an upset in the other semi as the U.S. were beaten 4-0 by underdogs Brazil. To put this in context, this was the year of Marta, and the Brazilian legend scored two of those goals. Despite Marta's brilliance, Germany were the world's dominant force right now and beat Brazil in the final to win their second World Cup in a row. Marta won the Golden Boot with seven goals and the Golden Ball for best player. All teams received financial bonuses for the first time at the 2007 Women's World Cup according to the round they reached. The Champions won one million U.S. dollars, and those exiting at the first round received a cash boost of $200,000. Obviously, this wasn't even vaguely comparable with the men's competition, but it was massive progress.

English football made historic progress too when, better late than never, Lily Parr, the iconic Dick, Kerr Ladies player who took women's football by storm way back in the 1920s, was inducted into the National Football Museum's Hall of Fame in 2002. Finally, an acknowledgement that women were part of footballing history, even if they had spent decades being cancelled. It was an acknowledgement of all that had gone before and a strong hint that perceptions were changing.

Profile: Marta

Marta is considered the best-ever female player. With 115 goals for her country and 17 World Cup goals — a record across the women's and men's games — it's hard to dispute. She was the first player to score at five different World Cups and five different Olympics. Born in 1986, Marta is Brazilian-Swedish and has played at club level in both countries. Aged 14, her talent was uncovered, and shortly after, she began her career with Vasco de Gama in Rio de Janeiro. In 2004, she moved to Sweden to play for Umeå IK. The same year, she was awarded the Golden Ball for best player at the FIFA Under-19s Women's World Championship. During her five years at Umeå, she scored 111 goals in 103 appearances and won seven league titles. She played in the U.S. and Sweden again, before returning to Orlando Pride in 2017, where she still plays. During her career, she's won FIFA World Player of the Year six times, five of them consecutively between 2006-2010. Her flair, skill, and creativity have earned her the title of the greatest of all time. FIFA honoured this legacy in 2024 by awarding her their Special Award at the annual The Best FIFA Football Awards. They also created a new award in her honour for the best goal scored in women's football each year. It's known as the "Marta Award".

12

The 2010s: Evolution

League Developments

We're very close to modern times here, but the changes we've
seen across women's football within this decade and the first few
years of the next are incredible. It was a slow start for women
in football — battling the ban, facing continual opposition, and
actively having the game's growth suppressed in most countries
— but finally, nearly 100 years after the introduction of the
ban, widespread changes were happening. The most significant
change in England (and a significant one across the world if you
consider the impact changes in England have on football) was
the establishment of England's Women's Super League (WSL) in
2011.

When the WSL was announced in 2009, 16 clubs applied for the
initial eight places. In 2011, when it was introduced, the eight
teams in the first WSL were Arsenal, Birmingham City, Bristol
Academy, Chelsea, Doncaster Rovers Belles, Everton, Lincoln
Ladies, and Liverpool. It began as a summer league, which ran

from April until October, rather than the standard winter league (September to May), and for the first two seasons, there was no relegation out of the WSL. Chelsea and Arsenal kicked off the new league on April 13th, 2011, and Arsenal won the opening game, watched by 2,500 people. Gilly Flaherty scored the first WSL goal, and a few months later, Arsenal won their first WSL title. The following season, they added their second title. With their league and cup experience built up since the team began in 1987, Arsenal remained the best team in the country. Now there was professional football available in their home country, English players who had been playing in the United States came home. Among them were Alex Scott and Kelly Smith, who had been playing with the Boston Breakers but returned to rejoin the now professional Arsenal team. The Women's Super League began to attract the best players in the world. In 2013, the Professional Football Association (PFA) granted full membership to all women playing in the WSL, to cement professionalism in the league. It also launched the first PFA Women's Players' Player of the Year award (won by Arsenal's Kim Little). In 2014, WSL2 was introduced as a second division. Ten teams competed in the second tier, and for the first time, there was a relegation from WSL1 (which it was called) to WSL2.

However, undermining the new professionalism was a controversial decision. Doncaster Rovers Belles (the legendary team of the 1980s and 1990s) were told they would be relegated from WSL1 to WSL2. It didn't matter what position they finished at the end of the season; they would be the team to be relegated. The Belles had been in the top flight of women's football for 22 years and were one of the most iconic teams in the world. They had showcased the game when the FA weren't supportive, and they were one of the few teams the public had heard of, thanks to their regular visibility in the FA Cup Final. But, ignoring the accepted rules of promotion and relegation, the FA decided the Belles were to be relegated even if they won the league. Absolute insanity. Would that happen in the men's game? It was described as "morally scandalous" by Vik Akers, Arsenal's manager. And I'm sure a few other words were said about the decision, too. Manchester City Ladies were to replace the Doncaster Rovers Belles in the WSL1. The reason? Manchester City had more money. The Belles were not invited to compete for a place in the new WSL1, despite having won the FA Cup six times in their history, because they didn't have the financial backing. The Donny Belles appealed, but the FA again showed their disregard for women's football and upheld their decision to relegate them based on money rather than achievement. For all the positives gained from a professional league, the English FA's decision left a very sour taste.

Over the next two years, WSL1 expanded from eight to ten teams, and, for the first time, there was promotion from the third tier FA Women's Premier League into WSL2, meaning the WSL divisions were now linked to the rest of the football pyramid for the first time. In 2017, to bring the women's league in line with the men's league, the FA moved to a traditional winter league format away from the previous summer league — a sign that women's football was no longer seen as a sideshow.

The WSL became a full-time professional league for the first time in September 2018. The second tier became the FA Women's Championship, a semi-professional league that included some fully professional teams. To play in the professional WSL division, teams had to apply for a new full-time professional licence because clubs now had to offer a minimum of 16 hours a week contract and form a youth academy. The first entirely professional Women's Super League featured Arsenal, Birmingham City, Brighton & Hove Albion, Bristol City, Chelsea, Everton, Liverpool, Manchester City, Reading, West Ham United, and Yeovil Town. The new FA Women's Championship included eleven more teams who had to meet part-time criteria. Possibly the most significant step forward for women's football in England in the 2018/19 season was the reintroduction of a Manchester United Women's team, a team that hadn't existed since 2005. Manchester United's brand is massive, and a women's team would help raise the sport's profile both within and outside of England. The newly formed Manchester United Women began in the Championship division and were promoted, alongside Tottenham Hotspur, to the expanded WSL the following season. The league expanded to 12 teams, helped by Barclays investment, the biggest sponsorship investment ever into a UK women's sport.

Although development in Scotland was slower, the Scottish Premier League expanded and reorganised in 2016, adding a second division — SWPL2. The first professional contracts were signed in the SWPL when Lauren Evans and Lauren Coleman put pen to paper for the second tier (SWPL2) team Glasgow Women (a different team to Glasgow City). The Scottish national team reached an all-time high FIFA world ranking of 19th in 2014 as more players played their club football in the more competitive English leagues. The national team also qualified for their first major tournament in 2017 when they qualified for the Euros. The following year, they qualified for their first World Cup finals, and in recognition of the achievement, the Scottish government funded the team to allow the players the chance to train full-time for the six months leading up to the tournament. Nearly 140 years since the first recorded meeting between Scotland and England, football was finally being recognised in Scotland. The Scottish TV broadcaster BBC Alba announced in 2019 that they would regularly begin broadcasting SWPL1 matches. Glasgow Rangers started introducing professional contracts for the first time (which encouraged other teams to follow). In Scotland's final game before the World Cup, 18,555 people came out to watch their friendly against Jamaica. To add the icing to the 2010s cake, Claire Emslie scored Scotland's first World Cup goal in 2019, albeit in their defeat against England: the rivalry continues.

Several years ahead of England's WSL, the U.S. founded the fully professional National Women's Soccer League (NWSL) in 2012. After several unsuccessful attempts, this new league was set up under the ownership of the teams. The first eight investor-operator teams were Boston Breakers, Chicago Red Stars, FC Kansas City, Portland Thorns, Seattle Reign FC, Sky Blue FC, Washington Spirit, and Western New York Flash (again, a minute for the cool names). Kansas City and Portland Thorns played the first match in April 2013, and Portland went on to win the league. The league was largely successful, and new teams joined (Houston Dash,

Orlando Pride), changed contracts from one team to another (Western New York Flash to North Carolina College and Kansas City to Utah Royals), rebranded (Seattle Reign FC to Reign FC), or folded (Boston Breakers) before the end of the decade. Whatever the teams, established names and players freshly out of college could now play professional football again.

The national team continued to win and, through the decade, won two more World Cups (2015 and 2019) and their fourth Olympic gold medal at London 2012. Over a two-year period between 2012 and 2014, the team recorded a 43-game unbeaten streak. Despite continually winning major trophies, the USWNT still wasn't being treated fairly by U.S. Soccer, though. In 2016, some of its stars sued the Equal Opportunities Commission to demand equal pay to their men's team. Let's be honest, the men's team are not even on the radar of most major tournaments, so why should they be paid more than the hugely successful women's team? There is no argument except discrimination. Hope Solo, Carli Lloyd, Alex Morgan, Megan Rapinoe, and Beck Sauerbrunn, some of the biggest names in the sporting world, used their position to demand more for players. They didn't secure equal pay at this point but did get improved wages and match bonuses. A few years later, in 2019, most of the U.S. team filed a gender discrimination case asking for equal pay, equal training facilities, and equal travel conditions (the men flew first class whilst the women did not). After a long fight, U.S. Soccer settled the lawsuit in February 2022 and finally agreed on equal pay. Once again, the team had moved the story on, and other national teams began considering their position on equality.

Many leagues across the world were becoming more professional by the end of the decade. However, the term "professional" is used loosely and includes semi-professional, some players with professional contracts, or a fully professional team. For example, some of Manchester City's players were given professional contracts in 2014, and Chelsea went fully professional in 2015, but their Women's Super League only required all teams to be fully professional (and pay a salary to every player) from 2018. England's WSL was the first in Europe to become fully professional, but most other leagues in Europe were still semi-professional, with a smattering of professional clubs. For example, despite offering semi-professional conditions in Italy in the 1970s, Serie A still wasn't fully professional; Barcelona's women's team went professional in 2015, but Spain's Liga F wasn't, and Lyon were professional, but the French D1F wasn't. As professionalism was being introduced into leagues across Europe, other positive shifts were happening too. For example, French referee Stéphanie Frapport took charge of the Women's World Cup final in 2019 for the first time and refereed major high-profile men's games. Attitudes and opportunities for women were finally changing.

It wasn't just in Europe. Across the world, leagues were becoming professionalised to varying degrees. In 2015, the Chinese FA recognised there was a problem with their national team's competitiveness on the world scene and relaunched the Women's Super League. They negotiated sponsorship deals, introduced a second division, and, with further investment, could increase player salaries and recruit top players from all over the world. The Chinese Women's Super League was born in a bid to professionalise the sport for women. There were eight teams at the top level of the Super League and a second division of another eight teams, which allowed for promotions and relegations. A development plan was put in place to help improve China's performance on the international scene, and commercial partners and TV broadcasters supported the Women's Super League. In 2016, the league went fully professional.

In 2013, Brazil's first women's league was formed. The Copa do Brasil de Futebol Feminino was contested briefly before being scrapped to make way for the Campeonato Brasileiro de Futebol Feminino (Brazilian Women's National Championship). In 2017, the league was restructured to give a 16-team Série A1, a 16-team Série A2, and later, in 2021, a 32-team Série A3. In 2019, the Brazilian Women's National Championship became Brazil's first national professional women's league.

The establishment was changing too, and in 2018, the first Women's Ballon d'Or was introduced. In men's football, the Ballon d'Or has been awarded annually since 1956, so introducing a women's best player in the world award was a long overdue advancement for world football. The French magazine *France Football* gives the award to honour the player who is considered the best in the world over the previous season. It's prestigious and a big deal, although it is still plagued with sexist undertones since the award ceremony is held during the women's winter international break, so most female players can't attend because they have national team camps scheduled. Beth Mead has described it as a "tick box" event, and Jen Beattie of Arsenal and Scotland said those involved needed to "do better" — a reminder there is still much work to be done. Ada Hegerberg of Norway was announced as the first winner of the prestigious award, Megan Rapinoe won in 2019, and Spain's Alexia Putellas (2021 and 2022) and Aitana Bonmati (2023 and 2024) have both won it twice. Between 2018 and 2023, Australia's Sam Kerr and France's Wendie Renard were the only players to be nominated every year, and in 2023, Mary Earps became the highest-ranking goalkeeper when she came fifth.

Major international competitions come around at least every two years now, including the World Cup, the Olympics, and the federation championships such as the Euros. With developing leagues, it allowed national sides to see how their investment translated on the biggest stages. Tournaments had become less predictable as teams got stronger, and there was a distinct air of change in Europe, and indeed the world, as more teams became competitive. Visibility grew, quality grew, and so, demand grew.

Major Tournaments

Germany hosted the first major tournament of the decade, the 2011 World Cup. By now, the tournament was big business, and television coverage was unprecedented. Local broadcasters showed all the games, and the production values and camera angles improved significantly. Matches were televised across the world. It was also the first tournament where the sticker manufacturer Panini produced stickers of the Women's World Cup stars. The strength in depth of football was evident, too, as two of the quarter-finals were decided on penalties, and Japan knocked out hosts Germany. Japan beat Sweden to reach their first World Cup final, where they faced the U.S. They'd already upset Germany. Surely they couldn't beat the U.S. too?

The 48,817 spectators in Frankfurt waited until the 69th minute of the final before United States' star forward Alex Morgan fired home. Then, 12 minutes later, Japan equalised through Aya Miyama, and the game went to extra time. The U.S. again took the lead, this time when one of their greatest ever players, Abby Wambach, hit the back of the net. Unfazed by the star quality on the other side of the pitch, though, Japan equalised again, this time through their own star, Homare Sawa. Penalties were needed to decide the 2011 title. Uncharacteristically, the Americans struggled. They missed their first three penalties whilst the Japanese players kept their nerve. After years of investment and learning their craft, Japan lifted their first World Cup trophy. A surprise result maybe, but Japan had been putting in the work ever since they hosted the 1981 Mundialito to learn from the best teams in Europe. Their dedication had paid off.

The London 2012 Olympics gave another opportunity for England and the rest of the UK teams to showcase their sport in front of a home crowd. But there was one problem. There is no England, Scotland, Wales, or Northern Ireland team at the Olympics; it's a Great Britain team, so the individual football nations couldn't play. Since hosting the Olympics is a massive deal, an agreement was reached by the individual nations to form a Great Britain football team for the first time (after some resistance from the Scottish FA). Hope Powell, England's manager, was

Profile: Homare Sawa

Homare Sawa is arguably the greatest Asian player of all time. Born in 1978, she began her playing career aged 12 for Nippon TV Beleza where she played between 1991 and 1999. She won five titles and scored 79 goals in 136 appearances for them. She moved to the U.S. to play, before returning to Japan in 2004. Homare's career spanned 24 years, and her international career spanned 22 of them. As captain of Japan, she oversaw their meteoric rise to global glory. At the 2008 Beijing Olympics, Japan finished fourth and Homare finished as the third-highest scorer, sharing the honour with Marta.

At the 2011 FIFA Women's World Cup, she scored a hat-trick against Mexico: the oldest player to score a World Cup hat-trick. In extra time of the 2011 final, Homare scored the equaliser to keep Japan in the game. She finished the tournament as top scorer. Later that year, she was named FIFA Women's Player of the Year — the first Asian, man or woman, to win the title. In 2012, Homare Sawa captained Japan to a silver medal at the London Olympics. Although she retired after the tournament, she came out of retirement to represent her country one last time at the 2015 World Cup (her sixth World Cup). Soon after, she retired for good. Still Japan's most-capped player, she scored 83 goals (also a record) in 205 games. In 2014, she was among the first inductees to the Asian Football Hall of Fame.

asked to select the best squad for the job, regardless of the individual nation they usually represent. The final squad was made up of 16 English players and two Scottish players, and the players realised dreams they had never thought possible. Twelve teams competed in the London Olympics, including the first-ever Great Britain football team. It was an enormous deal for the players. The Olympics had never been on the cards before. For Rachel Brown-Finnis, who was towards the end of her career, making the squad was essential.

"Six months before selection, I'm seven knee operations in at this point. I said I need to just lay everything else to the side and try to do everything to get in this Olympic squad. I quit work in September 2011 to make sure I could rest if I needed to rest, put my feet up, rehab, ice my knee, game ready my knee, everything I could do to make sure that training was my priority and then, ultimately, training was getting ready for game time and the performance was my priority. I was so proud of myself for getting to the Olympics, to making that squad. I remember standing on that balcony at Wembley Stadium when we'd beaten Brazil 1-0, looking at Wembley Way filtering out and I just thought this is pretty much 25 years on from when I'd been that little kid inspired and being in that swell of a crowd down Wembley Way [watching Burnley men play Wolves in 1988] and I could never have imagined that I would be stood here as part of team GB as part of a virtually sell out Wembley. I didn't dream of that because I just never thought it was even within the reach of dreams, let alone reality."

Team GB didn't waste the opportunity and beat all three teams in their group, one of whom was Brazil, featuring Marta, the best player in the world. Their final group game against Brazil brought 70,584 people to Wembley to watch. The Team GB players became household names, particularly Steph Houghton, who scored goals in each group game despite being a defender. Great Britain topped their group but were knocked out by Canada in the quarter-finals. France, Japan, Canada, and the U.S. made it through to the semi-finals. Japan beat France before an epic seven-goal game between Canada and the U.S., where an Alex

Morgan goal three minutes into stoppage time at the end of extra time put the United States through to the final. The U.S. beat Japan to win gold (their fourth), and Canada got the bronze medal. More importantly, for the health of the sport, attendance figures during the Games were huge. Nearly 661,000 people watched the 26 matches, an average of 25,423 per match.

They may not have reached the tournament's later stages, but by the time Team GB were knocked out, they'd further ignited support for women and girls playing football. Again, the footballing authorities took note, and in 2013, The FA, Sport England, The Premier League, and The Football League Trust launched a national programme to get girls into football and give them opportunities to play. The legacy of the London 2012 Games was talked about a lot; getting more girls into football was one of those legacy moments.

It was back to the Euros in 2013 for England, and after raising their profile at the Olympics, there was more support than ever from their home fans. There was more support, full stop, for the tournament. After just one round of the group stage of the 2013 Euros in Sweden, overall ticket sales exceeded the total sold throughout the entire 2009 tournament. Over 40,000 people watched the first six games, including a sold-out crowd for Sweden's opener against Denmark. To acknowledge the increased interest in the game, UEFA introduced fan zones at matches for the first time. The standard of play matched the demand for tickets, as investment improved quality on the field (unsurprisingly, people get better when they can train as professionals). The tournament director at the 2013 Euros, Göran Havik, said it was the best women's football he'd seen. He described Spain's 3-2 win over England in their opening group game as "technically brilliant at times. We got to see a very high-quality game." Alright, no need to sound so surprised.

England were seeded fourth for the 2013 Euros, so expectations were high even though they were without their all-time leading goal scorer, Kelly Smith, for most of the competition. And as Mr Havik described, the opening game was a thriller. Spain scored within four minutes, but England had pegged them back a few minutes later. It remained 1-1 until the 85th minute when Spain went ahead again through Jenni Hermoso. A minute from time, Laura Bassett equalised for England. Just as it looked like ending as a draw, Alexia Putellas scored four minutes into stoppage time to give Spain all three points. It was a tough start for the Lionesses but a win for women's football. Unfortunately, England finished bottom of their group and Hope Powell's position as head coach hung in the balance. Meanwhile, it was back to the usual suspects in the last four as Germany and the Nordic countries rose to the top once more. In front of a record crowd of 41,301 people, Germany won their eighth title (sixth in a row) when they beat Norway. More attendance records were set, and 216,888 tickets were sold throughout the tournament, giving an average match attendance of 8,676.

After the Lionesses disappointing Euro campaign, Hope Powell, their coach of 15 years and the woman who helped build the game to new levels, was sacked by the FA. A few months later, her replacement, Mark Sampson, was appointed the new manager. In March 2015, England won the Women's Cyprus Cup (for the third time). And then came the 2015 World Cup.

The appetite for the World Cup continued to increase, and an average of 26,000 spectators watched each of the 52 matches at the newly expanded Canada World Cup. The number of teams increased from 16 to 24, and eight teams made their debut: Cameroon, Costa Rica, Ecuador, Ivory Coast, Netherlands, Spain, Switzerland, and Thailand. Another addition to this World Cup was goal-line technology, the first time it was used at the women's event. A less popular addition was artificial pitches, which had never been used in a World Cup before. This bizarre idea led to a sex discrimination lawsuit against FIFA and the Canadian Soccer Association when a group of people, including some of the world's best footballers, came together to question why the authorities considered it acceptable for women to play their top international competition on synthetic grass rather than actual grass. They argued that artificial pitches play completely differently from grass pitches and pose injury risks that grass does not. The tournament continued on the artificial grass, showing there was still some way to go before women's and men's football were considered equals. It also showed that players stood up for their game and saw activism as part of their role as the current custodians of the sport.

Since receiving investment, England began to show promise at major events again, and the 2015 World Cup was a watershed moment for the modern Lionesses. They finished their group as

runners-up to France and faced Norway, a traditionally excellent
side, in the Round of 16. Goals from Steph Houghton and Lucy
Bronze secured a 2-1 win. Next, they faced the hosts, Canada.
They beat them, too. English fans were beginning to dream.

For the first time in their history, the Lionesses had reached the
semi-finals of the FIFA World Cup. Germany, Japan, and the U.S.,
all previous winners, also reached the semis. England played Japan,
the defending champions. As all English hearts are somewhat used
to, it was a heartbreaking end to the tournament. Japan took the
lead, but several minutes later, Fara Williams levelled up from the
penalty spot. It remained 1-1 until 90+2 minutes. Then a cruel and
unfortunate own goal broke English hearts. Devastating. Germany
lost their semi-final to the U.S., so the European rivals played
the third-place play-off match. During extra time, Fara Williams
scored a penalty to win third place for England in the 2015 World
Cup. It was a massive achievement for the Lionesses. The result
was celebrated nationwide, and the players became household
names. Most importantly, more girls were inspired to play football,
helping to find the stars of the future. The BBC showed every
game for the first time, and Rachel Yankey, Rachel Brown-Finnis,
and Sue Smith — all ex-England players — formed part of the
presenting and commentary teams.

Women's football had properly broken through in the UK for the
first time.

[Author's note: I remember watching as much as I could of
this World Cup. Having spent decades watching as many of the
men's major tournaments as I could, it felt good to finally watch

the women's equivalent. I remember watching that third-place play-off and the utter joy when England won it, making household names of the players. It was the first time that the nation really got behind the women's team. Something had shifted in England.]

Meanwhile, in the final, the U.S. got their revenge on Japan to secure their third world title. England's third-place finish was arguably more important to the game as a whole, though, as now there was another team fighting for the top spots. There had long been criticism of the quality of football and the strength in depth of teams in the World Cup, so with every new contender, every new country investing in their women's pathway, the sport grew stronger.

The Olympics in Rio in 2016 brought a major international women's football competition to Brazil for the first time. It also brought a surprise when Sweden knocked the U.S. out in the quarter-finals after a penalty shootout. It was the first time the USWNT had failed to reach at least the semi-finals of a major event since the UEFA, FIFA, and Olympic events began. Instead, Brazil, Sweden, Canada, and Germany reached the semi-finals, none of whom were strangers to the later stages of competitions. Sweden and Germany reached the final and Germany won their first Olympic gold medal. Canada won the bronze, breaking home hearts by beating Brazil. The final in the Maracaña in Rio was watched by 52,432 people, bringing the sport and the talents of superstar Marta and her colleagues to a broader audience. When the 2017 Euros came around, expectations were high for England after their breakthrough display at the 2015 World Cup. People

in the street now knew more about them, and general interest in
the tournament rose. More generally, the twelfth UEFA Women's
Euros, held in the Netherlands, was played against a backdrop
of increasing strength and depth in the sport. With more teams
ready to compete and a clear increase in demand, the competition
expanded from 12 to 16 teams. The expansion allowed new teams
to compete against the best in Europe, and Scotland, Belgium,
Austria, Portugal, and Switzerland all made their Euros debuts.
The total prize money also reflected the growth, increasing from
2.2 million Euros in 2013 to 8 million in 2017. As competition
in Europe increased, it became harder to predict who would win.
Nobody was betting against Germany to pick up another trophy,
but matches were getting closer. As the quality and the drama
increased, so did the popularity of the sport. And there was going
to be drama and unpredictability this time around.

Scotland qualified for the Euros tournament for the first time
in their history. It was a landmark moment for Scottish football,
built on a solid foundation of improvement over recent years.
Unfortunately, they were drawn in a group with England, who
beat them easily, but Scotland picked up a big win against Spain
and narrowly lost to Portugal. They finished on three points,
the same as both Spain and Portugal, but due to their goal
difference, Scotland finished third in the group and just missed
out on qualifying for the knockout stages in their first-ever major
tournament. It was an excellent effort but a disappointing end.
Erin Cuthbert scored Scotland's first-ever Euro goal, and Shelley
Kerr became the first manager to take the team to a major
tournament.

It was a tournament of debutant heroics, as Austria beat France
to top their group before beating Spain on penalties in the
quarter-finals. Austria reached the semi-finals of the Euros in their
first competition. There had been a shift in the standard of football
across Europe, but could anyone topple the Germans? The short
answer is yes. England, the Netherlands, and Denmark reached
the semi-finals alongside Austria. Germany, who had won six titles
in a row (a 22-year dominance), were knocked out by Denmark
in the quarter-finals. It was a huge upset and another sign the
standard of football had increased throughout the continent.
England faced the Netherlands in the semi-final, who in their
home tournament, were on a mission to show how far the Dutch
women's team had developed under head coach Sarina Weigman.
England were the top-ranked team left in the tournament and had
high hopes. Their hopes were challenged when, twenty minutes in,
Vivianne Miedema scored the opening goal. Mistakes by England
led to Daniëlle Van de Donk adding a second in the second half.
England missed chances and made mistakes throughout, and the
Dutch calmly and cleverly went about their business. A stoppage
time England own goal summed up the result, and the English
Lionesses' roar was quietened. The Dutch Lionesses, however,
made it to their first final. Meanwhile, newbies Austria lost out on
penalties to Denmark, but what a run for the newcomers.

The final was fast-paced and exhilarating. Denmark went in front
shortly after kick-off from a penalty, but a few minutes later,
the outstanding Vivianne Miedema equalised. Two more goals
came before half-time, and it was level 2-2 at the break. In the
second half, the Netherlands came out flying. They scored a third

shortly after the break and sealed it with a fourth just before the final whistle. The hosts won their first Euros trophy, and so did head coach Sarina Weigman. The overall attendance record was a winner too, thanks to the increase in the number of matches now more teams were involved. A total of 247,041 fans attended.

England finished Euro 2017 disappointed but had again captured the nation's hearts at home. Broader cultural changes around women's football were happening in England, suggesting the landscape was changing too. At Deepdale, Preston North End's ground where the Dick, Kerr Ladies sometimes played, a memorial was unveiled to commemorate 100 years since the first game, listing all the women who ever played for the factory team. Another example was a blue plaque put on the wall of the Preston factory that was home of the Dick, Kerr Ladies to commemorate all they had done to promote the game and make it visible. The plaque was a first for women's football. These two signs suggested that the sport's history was finally being "uncancelled" in England.

Although we're into recent history, development has snowballed during the past few years. There has been increasing visibility across the world, increasing interest, and continued conversation about creating a more equal landscape for women footballers. But governing bodies were still causing controversy.

The 2019 Women's World Cup was the first to use VAR (Video Assistant Referee) — but it wasn't this rule change that attracted the headlines, or at least not on its own. A matter of days before the tournament started, The International Football Association Board (IFAB), responsible for the laws of the game, introduced a new goalkeeper rule for penalties. FIFA decided the Women's World Cup was an acceptable guinea pig to test a brand new law, something that is usually reserved for less high-stakes competitions. The new rule was that goalkeepers needed to keep at least one foot on the goal line when a penalty was taken, a completely new rule. It represented a massive disadvantage to goalkeepers who had only a few days' notice to change how they had prepared themselves for penalties for their entire careers.

Having introduced it, FIFA then used VAR to police it, right down to deviations of the smallest margins. It affected games. At a World Cup. Goalkeepers were booked if the rule was broken by the smallest of margins, and penalties were retaken if the penalty taker didn't score on the first attempt. It negatively affected the game. It was a shambles. The rule change was heavily criticised amid claims that FIFA did not take the women's game seriously enough. Would that have happened in the men's World Cup? Many players and coaches didn't think it would and branded the decision as sexist. Halfway through the tournament, FIFA backtracked and asked IFAB to temporarily suspend the new law, meaning goalkeepers would not be booked for breaking the rule. The suspension was granted, and IFAB and FIFA both looked a bit silly.

Penalty controversy aside, though, the 2019 France World Cup provided plenty of good entertainment and large audiences. Over a billion people worldwide watched the tournament, and over 82 million viewers watched the final — a new record. A fun fact from FIFA's figures: by the time England and Scotland had finished their group stage matches, exactly 50% of potential UK viewers had watched at least one minute of the tournament.

Scotland qualified for the World Cup for the first time, continuing to make history. Unfortunately, they were again drawn in a group with England. The result was much closer than last time, though, and Scotland only lost 2-1. Claire Emslie scored Scotland's first World Cup goal. England had a new manager by then, the untested Phil Neville, but he successfully steered them through the group stages by winning all three games.

For Scotland, it was a much tighter route to knockout stage qualification. Scotland needed to beat Argentina in their last group game to progress. The game was going well, and Scotland were 3-0 up after goals from Kim Little, Jen Beattie, and Erin Cuthbert. Cuthbert scored the third in the 69th minute and Scotland were just over 20 minutes away from getting through to the knockout phase of a World Cup. Five minutes later, Argentina scored one back and were encouraged. Another five minutes later, Argentina got lucky with a shot that hit the bar before coming off goalkeeper Lee Alexander and crossing the line. It was going to be a nervy finish for Scotland, and with just over ten minutes to go, they were clinging on at 3-2. And then disaster struck. The video assistant referee (VAR) awarded a late penalty to Argentina, deep into time added on. Lee Alexander saved it but was thought to be off her line when it was struck, and it had to be re-taken. A devastated Scotland could only look on in agony as the second attempt went in, and Scotland went home. Heart breaking.

Hosts France won their group without dropping a point and
beat Brazil in extra time to reach the quarter-finals. They were
stopped by the U.S. in front of a 45,000-strong crowd, so it was
England, the U.S., Sweden, and the Netherlands who reached
the semi-finals. If England could have chosen their semi-final
opponents from that list, the U.S. wouldn't have been at the
top of it, but unfortunately, they didn't get to choose. It was an
edge-of-the-seat game and a true test of how far England had come.
Christen Press scored for the U.S. after just 10 minutes, but within
another 10 minutes, Ellen White had equalised for England. Game
on. Just after the half-hour mark, the U.S. were in front again
when Alex Morgan scored. She celebrated by pretending to drink
a cup of tea — it riled up many England fans, me included. It
turned out to be the winning goal for the U.S. too, and England
were knocked out. Despite the disappointment, it was a big step
forward for the Lionesses, who had never reached the semi-finals
of a World Cup before and had contested a close game toe-to-toe
with the Americans. England couldn't pick themselves up from
the disappointment of the semi-final loss and lost the third-place
play-off to Sweden.

The U.S. met the Netherlands in the final, a Netherlands side
who had recently won the Euros. Expectations were high for the
Dutch team, but they came up against a very strong U.S. side
and lost 2-0. The U.S. lifted the World Cup for the fourth time,
and Sarina Weigman's team were left heartbroken. Nearly 58,000
attended the final and throughout the tournament, 1.1 million
people went to games, an average of 21,756 per match. Football
was still winning.

On the back of their performances in France, England raised
their profile at home even further and inspired the nation.
Ellen White's six goals at the tournament made her a household
name, and the interest in the Lionesses was now sky-high. A
friendly match (is that possible?) against Germany at Wembley
in November 2019 drew a crowd of 77,786 fans — me, my
husband, and our then seven-year-old son were among them.
The game's impact on me was part of my inspiration for writing
this book.

International Development

The U.S. and Germany were still dominant nations in world
football, but with increased competition, teams like England and
the Netherlands were challenging for trophies. As leagues and
investments increased in many countries, the difference in skill
levels reduced. For Germany, after reaching a 16-game unbeaten
streak in the World Cup, their run was halted in 2011 when Japan
beat them unexpectedly in the quarter-finals of the competition.
This also meant Germany didn't qualify for the 2012 Olympics
in London. Despite the setbacks, they were still at the top of the
European pile and bounced back to win their sixth straight title at
the 2013 Euros (helped by their goalkeeper Nadine Angerer, who
saved two penalties in the final against Norway). They reached the
semi-finals of the 2015 World Cup but were knocked out in the
2017 Euros by a resurgent Denmark. They reached the same stage
in the 2019 World Cup, this time beaten by Sweden, the first time
Sweden had beaten Germany in 24 years. Consequently, Germany
failed to qualify for the Olympics again, and after many years of

domination, the strength in depth across Europe and the world had started to challenge Germany.

Italy continued to struggle on the international stage, although they qualified for both the 2013 and 2017 Euros. By the end of the decade, things were looking up, and for the first time in 20 years, they qualified for the World Cup (2019). They qualified from their group and beat China in the Round of 16 but were knocked out by European Champions, the Netherlands, in the quarter-finals. Not unreasonably, the lack of a fully professional women's league has been blamed for the poor performances of the national side. Despite attracting women from across Europe in the 1970s with what was considered professional football (but would be considered semi-professional now), Serie A Femminile didn't turn fully professional until the 2022/23 season. As professional football for women develops, the national side hopes to become more competitive again.

The Dutch FA invested heavily in women's football towards the end of the noughties, and it soon showed on the international stage. Ten years after the start of the Eredivisie league (and the investment), the national team won their first major trophy. Winning on home soil increased the popularity of football in the country, and in 2019, they nearly upgraded their Euros trophy to a World Cup. On the back of this success, they played their first Olympics in 2020.

France's domestic league improved, too, and so did the national teams' performances. In 2010, the under-19s won their Euros, and in 2011, the senior team not only qualified for the World

Cup but finished in fourth place. France were now contenders. In 2012, they won the Cyprus Cup and came fourth at the Olympics. The under-19s again won their Euros in 2013 (and again in 2016 and 2019), whilst the senior team reached the Euros quarter-finals in 2013 and 2017. They reached the quarter-finals of their home-hosted 2019 World Cup campaign and were represented in the final when Stéphanie Frappart refereed the match between the U.S. and the Netherlands.

There was little to shout about if you followed the Spanish women's national team in the 2000s, but the 2010s brought a glimmer of hope. The national team waited until 2013 before qualifying for a major tournament but then reached the quarter-finals. In 2015, they qualified for their first World Cup, and within a few years, they would lift the trophy.

Canada began the decade with a new coach when the experienced Carolina Morace joined them. By February 2011, the team had risen to ninth in the world rankings. But continued disputes with the Canadian Soccer Association (CSA) over funding and compensation led Morace to announce she would quit after the 2011 World Cup. The team backed her and went on strike, so the Canadian Soccer Association began talks to resolve the dispute. They made promises to address the issues, and the players went back to the field with Morace, who took back her resignation. Sadly, it wasn't to be. Canada lost all three group games, and Morace resigned.

Incoming coach John Herdman then guided Canada to gold at the 2011 Pan American Games, followed by a bronze medal at

the 2012 London Olympics. Canada hosted the 2015 World Cup
with the dubious honour of being the first World Cup, female
or male, to be played on artificial pitches. The team won their
group and beat Switzerland in the Round of 16 before England
knocked them out. At the Olympics in Rio, Canada somewhat
made up for this disappointment by winning the bronze medal.
Brazil had reached the quarter-finals of the 2011 World Cup and
2012 Olympics, and the Round of 16 at the 2015 World Cup,
so understandably, expectations were high for a home Olympics
medal in 2016. They narrowly missed out on the bronze but had
had a solid decade in major tournaments. They reached the Round
of 16 at the 2019 World Cup too, which meant they had reached
the knockout stage of every major tournament that decade.

Australia built on the growth of its domestic game and produced
a national side that began challenging the rest of the world. In
2010, they started by winning the Women's Asian Cup and, by the
end of 2017, were ranked fourth in the world. They consistently
reached the knockout stages of the World Cup through the 2010s,
and towards the end of the decade, the Matildas were selling out
matches and setting attendance records. In New Zealand, the
senior team reached the Olympics' quarter-finals. In 2014, the
Under-20s reached the quarter-finals of the U20s World Cup, and
in 2018, the Under-17s finished third at their World Cup.

Japan's development into a world-class team reached its height
when they won the 2011 World Cup, the first Asian team to win
a senior FIFA event. They reached the final in 2015 too, but the

Profile: Christine Sinclair

Christine Sinclair is a legend of the game. Born in 1983, she only fully retired in 2024. She began playing at four in an Under-7s team and helped her team, Burnaby Girls, win six league titles. She was selected for the British Colombia under-14s team when she was only 11 and won three league titles with her secondary school team. When she was 15, the 1999 World Cup inspired her to follow her dream of playing for her country. Christine made her senior debut for Canada at the age of 16 at the Algarve Cup. Unfazed by the big occasion, she scored three goals across the tournament. She went to college in the U.S. and played for the University of Portland. In her first season, she scored 23 goals, the best record for a first-year across the whole division. In 2003, she represented Canada at the World Cup and also played in the FIFA under-19s Women's World Championships. She scored a record 10 goals, helping Canada finish as runners-up. Christine scored 190 goals in 331 games for Canada. In 2010, she was the first Canadian to score 100 goals for her country and beat the country's national team appearance record the same year. In 2021, she earned her 300th cap at the opening game of their Olympics campaign. In the semi-final, they beat the U.S. for the first time in 20 years. Canada won the gold medal on penalties. If you ask the internet who has scored the most international goals, it will likely say Cristiano Ronaldo. It's wrong. Christine Sinclair has 190; Ronaldo has a long way to go to catch her.

U.S. got their revenge with a convincing win in the final. On the other hand, China failed to qualify for the 2011 World Cup, the first time they didn't make it to the finals. They also failed to qualify for the Olympics for the first time in 2012 but reached the knockout stages of both the 2015 and 2019 World Cups.

Representing Africa were the Super Falcons (Nigeria), who continued to qualify for the World Cup (they have never failed to qualify during the competition's history). In 2011, Equatorial Guinea, who made their only appearance to date, joined them. In 2015, Cameroon and Côte d'Ivoire also qualified, and Cameroon qualified again in 2019. In 2012 and 2016, South Africa qualified for the Olympics, and in 2019, they qualified for their first World Cup. The strength in depth of women's football was spreading throughout Africa during the decade.

It's clear that by this point in history, football had become more competitive across the continents, and football associations and confederations were slowly seeing the potential of women playing football. New firsts arrived regularly as the decade ended, and the 2020s were about to bring an upward trajectory that nobody could have imagined, even after the positive progression through this decade.

13

The 2020s: Revolution

We're now into much more familiar historical territory, so you
may already know much of this. But I think it's important to
keep a check on the milestones in recent times because they've
come thick and fast and contrast the traditionally slow progress.
The game has gained new recognition in England since the 2022
Euros win, and the football landscape for women is changing daily.
But it's important to acknowledge that although we've come a
long way, much more must be done before women's football is
treated as equal to men's. There have been significant changes
and improved visibility, but this is only the start. Infrastructure,
facilities, health, and mental wellbeing needs must all be addressed
in every country to bring gender equality to all those who play.
Wages, building an engaged fanbase, supporting players to have
families, etc., should all be part of future discussions. We must
continue to encourage girls to participate in sports, provide safe
and supported environments to learn, and banish the prejudice
of the past. This extends to coaching, refereeing, physios, and the
whole environment around football, from grassroots to elite level,
giving women and girls more opportunities to be part of the game.

In 2020, the English FA announced 3.4 million girls and women were playing football, a 54% increase since 2017. In 2021, the Let Girls Play campaign launched, normalising girls and women being sporty, and the WSL celebrated its tenth anniversary. And then there was 2022: an undeniably important year in the history of women's football in England and a catalyst for further growth across the world.

As hosts of Euro 2022, England hoped to put their disappointment at the 2005 event (which they also hosted) behind them. In their opening group game, they started slowly against Austria, but something felt different. A commanding display against Norway saw England score eight goals, including a hat-trick for Beth Mead, plus goals from four other players. The Lionesses then beat Northern Ireland 5-0. Germany were storming on too, winning all three of their group games. England's quarter-final opponents were Spain, a tough test but could it be a defining moment in English football? It was a game to remember. Spain controlled possession and frustrated England throughout, and ten minutes after half-time, Esther González scored for Spain. It looked like it was all over for England as time ticked by and Spain kept possession like only Spain can. But Sarina Weigman had used her substitutes well throughout the tournament, and this game was no exception. On came Ella Toone, who scored six minutes before the end to take the game to extra time. It remained cagey throughout (and stressful if you were an England or Spain fan), but a 96th-minute screamer from Georgia Stanway was enough to send the Lionesses through. Germany, Sweden, and France also progressed to the semi-finals. England's game against

Sweden should have been another tough test, but after squeaking
past Spain, England had a new swagger. There was also a sense
of destiny building. It took a while to break the deadlock, but
England were 1-0 up at half-time. In the second half, the Lionesses
came out blazing and scored three more goals, including Alessia
Russo's now famous back heel. England had reached another
Euros final. Germany had beaten France in the other semi to set
up the ultimate final showdown: England vs Germany. Could
England change their final day fortunes?

The Wembley-hosted final was played in front of a record crowd
of 87,192 fans. It was another tight match. And it was Toone
again who came off the sub's bench to score for England — a
fearless chip. Naturally, the crowd went wild. But the celebrations
were short-lived as 15 minutes later, Lina Magull equalised for
Germany, taking the final to extra time. It was the tipping point
for England fans between destiny and familiar heartbreak. But
as penalties loomed, Chloe Kelly poked home the winner for
England. She celebrated by emulating Brandi Chastain at the 1999
World Cup, whipping her shirt off and twirling it around her head.
It was an iconic celebration in 1999 and remained so in 2022. It
felt right to have the same celebration, bookending an important
phase for women's football. The U.S. World Cup tournament and
team of 1999 opened the door for women's football in modern
times; the England tournament and team of 2022 slammed the
door on past prejudice. It was a beautiful moment that sparked
considerable changes in the availability of football for girls in
England.

But this book is about the struggles as well as the triumphs. In the wake of the celebrations immediately after the match, BBC presenter Alex Scott was as emotional as the rest of us, maybe more so as she'd been part of the struggle. Amongst her words that night, she talked about how difficult it had been to get clubs to agree to use their stadiums for the matches. Speaking to BBC co-presenter Gabby Logan, Alex said,

"Let's just remind ourselves as well, back in 2018, we were begging people to host in their stadiums a women's game for this Euros. So many people said no. I hope you are all looking at yourselves right now because you weren't brave enough to see what it could have been."

Those words tell a story of where football was in England in terms of support, even so recently. Since then, things have started to change, and the Euros win has been the catalyst that people like Alex Scott knew it could be.

In every way, the 2022 Euros were bigger than previous versions. Across the 31 games, 574,875 attended matches: more than double who watched the previous Euros in the Netherlands. The average attendance per match was 18,544, nearly 10,000 more than the previous highest average in Sweden in 2013. Sixty broadcasters partnered with UEFA to televise the tournament. Those countries without a broadcaster deal could still watch coverage on the UEFA website. The tournament was watched live by 365 million people in 195 territories. According to UEFA's report, 84% of spectators said the tournament had improved their perception of women's football, and 88% were likely to watch a future professional international or domestic women's football event on TV. The figures are staggering. England's Euro 2022 literally changed the game.

In England, the Lionesses accelerated the growth of women's football beyond what could have been imagined before the Euros win. The legacy of that win changed the footballing landscape. The players themselves had an impact off the field, too, when they wrote to the UK government demanding equal access to sports for girls and boys in school physical education lessons. The government agreed. According to UEFA, over 416,000 new opportunities were created nationwide, in schools, clubs, and the community for women and girls in grassroots football. Baroness Sue Campbell, director of women's football at The FA and UEFA Women's 2022 board member, said after the tournament,

"Our aim for this tournament was twofold: to deliver a record-breaking tournament and to leave a tangible legacy to grow the women's game."

Job done.

In February 2023, England won the invitational Arnold Clark Cup for the second time, and the success of the Euros meant tens of thousands of fans came out to watch the matches across England, making top-level football accessible to a broader audience. The tournament was a major success. Women's football in England had never been more popular, and the Euros win translated into more spectators at WSL matches, too. As other countries have found, most notably the U.S., winning on the international stage doesn't necessarily mean people come out to watch domestic club matches. Without this audience watching games week after week, women's football cannot grow. In England, it was now growing. In April 2023, Wembley hosted the first ever Women's Finalissima, a further sign of progress from within the organisation of the game and another major moment. Finalissima is organised by UEFA and CONMEBOL — the South American Football Confederation — and played out between the winners of the most recent European and South American championships. For the first edition, this meant England faced Brazil. Over 83,000 fans came out to watch, and they were treated to a match with everything, including a penalty shootout to decide the winner. England won 4-2 when Euros hero Chloe Kelly calmly slotted the winning penalty home.

Already within the 2020s, the footballing landscape has changed so much for women. In England, and to some degree the rest of the United Kingdom, by hosting and winning the Euros in 2022, the Lionesses helped increase league attendance figures, participation, and media coverage. In 2023, Australia and New Zealand hosted the World Cup, giving them a chance to change the game in their home nations. And they did. The 2023 Women's World Cup was the most successful so far. The average match attendance was over 30,000, up nearly 10,000 on the 2019 tournament in France. In the UK, a peak audience of 12 million viewers watched on the BBC, more than for the men's Wimbledon final that year. In Spain, the highest-ever audience for a women's football match was recorded, and nearly 54 million people in China tuned in for their match against England, the highest TV audience for a single game. In Australia, Channel Seven, which broadcast the tournament, hit a record audience of over 11 million viewers, the most in its 20-year history. On top of stellar television viewing figures, over 1.9 million people watched matches at stadiums, an increase of around 75% on attendance at the previous tournament — mind-blowing. It was also the first Women's World Cup to break even financially, a big indicator of the future of the sport.

It didn't disappoint on the pitch either and was a brilliant advert for football at the highest level. The tournament expanded from 24 to 32 teams, and the prize pot increased from $30 million in 2019 to $110 million in 2023. According to FIFA, this was so every team and player could be financially supported. New Zealand won a World Cup match for the first time when they beat Norway in their opening game; the Republic of Ireland played their first ever World Cup match; the Jamaican and Colombian teams won people's hearts; but the U.S. were unexpectedly knocked out early after a penalty shoot-out with Sweden. Australia surprised everyone by knocking out France and Columbia, and the semi-final line-up consisted of Spain, Sweden, Australia, and England.

Spain and England reached the final, which was watched by over 75,000 people at Stadium Australia in Sydney. Spain won their first World Cup trophy. It was a huge triumph and should have been a joyous occasion for the players, but the aftermath showed that although football has come a long way, there is still so much more to be done for women in sport. Instead of enjoying the celebrations, the tournament ended in controversy when Spain's coach kissed a player on the lips without consent during the celebrations. The fallout was massive: across Spain, across football, and throughout the female community. Along the way, it uncovered some ugly practices behind the scenes in Spanish football. Rather than increase opportunities for girls, it showed that football may not be the type of environment parents wanted their daughters to be in. The team are considered "a golden generation" of Spanish players. A generation that it had been hoped would inspire positive change. But although Spain has broken into the FIFA top 10 rankings for the first time, won the World Cup, won the first Women's Nations League, and qualified for their first Olympic games in Paris (coming fourth), their success has not yet led to meaningful growth and development of the sport in their home country. There is still work to do to make football a safe place for females.

Towards the Future

At this point in history, there's so much to celebrate, as opportunities for girls and women increase throughout the globe. In 2020, Brazil's national women's team began receiving equal pay to the men's team — something that was unthinkable just a few decades ago. A country that traditionally believed women shouldn't play sports at all has now agreed that female national team players deserve the same pay as their male equivalents. In 2024, it was announced Brazil would host the 2027 Women's World Cup, the first South American country to do so. Again, given the Brazilian government made it illegal for women to play football until 1979, this is evidence of progress in society as well as in sports.

In Canada, Christine Sinclair scored her 185th international goal in 2020, beating Abby Wambach's record. Before she retired in 2023, Sinclair had scored 190 games in 328 matches for Canada, more than any other player, male or female (yep, including Cristiano Ronaldo, who, despite what the internet says, is still a long way behind). Her record may stand forever. The team reached a career-high in 2021 when they won the gold medal at the delayed Tokyo Olympics, and the future of football looks promising in Canada as a new professional league is due to start in the Spring of 2025. The Northern Super League will bring a professional women's domestic football league to Canada for the first time, and it's hoped the league will lead to meaningful change across the country. Six clubs will initially form the independently owned league, and the season will consist of 25 games plus play-offs. With teams from all over the country — Ottawa, Montreal, Toronto, Calgary, Vancouver, and Halifax — there is an opportunity to make the sport more visible to girls and women and provide greater opportunities. As a show of intent, the organisers deliberately left the word "women" from the league's title to show it is equal to other leagues. The sport continues to evolve.

In Africa, Morocco and Zambia made their World Cup debuts after reaching the 2023 event in Australia and New Zealand for the first time. In 2022, the Cup of Nations expanded from 8 teams to 12 and broke attendance records when Morocco played Nigeria in front of over 45,000 spectators. That year, South Africa won the title for the first time, and seasoned winners, Nigeria, finished fourth, showing how the depth of football in Africa is strengthening.

In France, the Ligue Féminine de Football Professional (LFFP) took over the running of the two top leagues on 1st July 2024. Both leagues are expected to become fully professional, and the LFFP hopes to extend the league in the future. With professionalisation, players should get improved facilities, including training centres for all teams, which the LFFP hopes will create one of the best leagues in the world. The new leagues are now known as the Première League and Seconde Ligue.

Switzerland, which will host the 2025 Euros, is already reaping the benefits of investing in a major tournament. Released tickets for Euros matches sold out quickly, and their first game against Australia, in October 2024, drew a record crowd of 14,370 to Zurich. It feels like Swiss football will soon benefit from the increased exposure a Euros competition will bring, too.

In England, the top two leagues, the Women's Super League and Women's Championship, are now owned and run by a new organisation, the Women's Professional Leagues Limited (WPLL). The English FA transferred ownership to the WPLL from the 2024/25 season, although it remains as a special shareholder. Each of the 24 clubs in the top two leagues are also shareholders and, with the organisation's help, will now focus on sustainably growing women's football in England. The Premier League has given the WPLL an interest-free loan, allowing them to build slowly and deliberately. When the leagues become profitable in the future, the FA will get a percentage of the profits to invest back into grassroots football for females: a complete cycle of growth and development. The WPLL has secured a new three-year sponsorship deal with Barclays Bank, double the previous investment, making it the biggest investment in women's domestic football history. Since the WPLL moved non-televised WSL games from the FA Player to YouTube this season, online viewing figures have soared, too. The myth that people don't watch women's football has now been completely debunked.

As viewing figures, match attendances, professionalism, and investment grow, we could be forgiven for thinking that the job is done. We've come a long way since Nettie Honeyball said, "If men can play football, so can women", but we mustn't get complacent; we're only getting started. For all the growth in recent years, there is still plenty to improve upon and fight for from grassroots to elite levels. Now, the work must continue: to get more girls into grassroots football, get more staying in the game, and provide them with clear pathways to success. More investment is needed to improve facilities and set up more clubs.

Then there's the work needed on injury prevention, which should start at the youth level and continue into the elite levels of the sport. With the increase in number of games played and the lack of investment into how to protect women's physiology, the number of serious injuries to players has spiralled. Anterior cruciate ligament (ACL) injuries are a constant threat to female players at every level. There has been much debate about how to tackle the ACL epidemic, and research and the application of this research must remain a top priority to ensure future generations are better protected. Specifically designed boots, negotiating TV deals for a different audience to the men's game, and continuing to provide a safe, family-friendly stadium environment are among many aspects of the game that need working out and refining.

Attitudes toward girls and women may have altered drastically since I was a kid dreaming of scoring at Wembley, but there are still pockets of sexism ready to burst out of the woodwork. During the summer of 2024 in England, there was a high-profile case where a grassroots club axed their girls' and women's teams because of a lack of club funds. Most of the all-male committee voted to disband the female teams to protect the male teams. There was a backlash on social media, including from high-profile Lionesses, and the committee later resigned. With the help of a more diverse committee, the female teams were reinstated.

Unfortunately, similar problems occur at the top of the game too, which poses a trickier problem to solve, given the money involved. Former WSL team Reading Women were victims of their club's financial mess recently, and the only way to keep the team together was for them to be relegated to the fifth tier of the football pyramid where they didn't need to invest money to meet the professional standards required at WSL and Women's Championship levels. It was devastating news. There is still a long way to go before things are truly fair.

Despite these frustrating and sad stories though, football for women and girls is now in a good place to grow. After over a century of battling, it finally feels like there is no going back, no chance that we could allow football to be cancelled again, and no chance we'll quietly step off the pitch. Whilst I, as a 10-year-old, had to dream of scoring a winner at Wembley as part of a men's team (which I would have totally smashed, by the way), today's girls have visible female role models on TV, in magazines, and across social media. The current players work tirelessly to make themselves available and visible to ensure these girls know they can play football. In the future, I hope to write an updated version of this book where true equality has been reached, but until then, let's celebrate the progress, push for the next steps, and enjoy the football.

What we see now is the tip of the iceberg: today's players are standing on the shoulders of many giants before them. I've talked about a few of these giants here to give you a flavour of how the story has evolved, but there are and were so many more people responsible for where the game is now. Maybe I'll talk about some of them in a future book. For now, to anyone who has ever helped football for girls and women to move forward, thank you.

Bonus Material

For bonus information that didn't make it into the final book, please visit:

www.theaccidentalcoach.co.uk/she-can-kick-it

Come and say hi on Instagram: @claremcwrites

References

Alegi, P. (2010). African Soccerscapes. How a Continent Changed the World's Game. [online] Google Books. Ohio: Ohio University Press. Available at: https://books.google.co.uk/books?id=NrW50yHkr0EC&printsec=frontcover&source=gbs_ge_summary_r&cad=0#v=onepage&q=women [Accessed 20 Sep. 2024].

Appleyard, I. (2017). Hope Powell leads tributes to D-Day veteran and former England women's football coach Martin Reagan. [online] York Press. Available at: https://www.yorkpress.co.uk/sport/15008670.D_Day_veteran_who_led_England_towards_a_new_footballing_era/ [Accessed 20 Sep. 2024].

BBC Scotland (2019). Banned by Scotland, so Rose won the World Cup with Italy instead. [online] BBC Scotland. Available at: https://www.bbc.co.uk/programmes/articles/1QZRzRJMZ4pyt9yRphyr8kt/banned-by-scotland-so-rose-won-the-world-cup-with-italy-instead [Accessed 20 Sep. 2024].

Brennan, P. (n.d.). Women's Football. [online] www.donmouth.co.uk. Available at: http://www.donmouth.co.uk/womens_football/womens_footb all.html [Accessed 20 Sep. 2024].

Byrne, H. (n.d.). Dictionary of Irish Biography - O'Brien, Anne Monica. [online] www.dib.ie. Available at: https://www.dib.ie/biography/obrien-anne-monica-a10287 [Accessed 20 Sep. 2024].

Campsie, A. (2021). Football legend Elsie Cook: 'I had to prove that women could play'. [online] The Scotsman. Available at: https://www.scotsman.com/news/national/football-legend-elsie-cook-i-had-to-prove-women-could-play-3491165 [Accessed 20 Sep. 2024].

Chapman, M. (2023). The first Football Fern: Barbara Cox and the struggle for female footballers. [online] The Spinoff. Available at: https://thespinoff.co.nz/sports/20-07-2023/the-first-football-fer n-barbara-cox-and-the-struggle-for-female-footballers [Accessed 20 Sep. 2024].

Critchley, M. (2019). VAR: England goalkeeper Karen Bardsley calls new penalty laws 'cruel and pedantic' after World Cup farce. [online] Independent. Available at: https://www.independent.co.uk/sport/football/womens_footba ll/var-penalty-retake-rules-laws-womens-world-cup-2019-englan d-goalkeeper-karen-bardsley-a8967831.html [Accessed 20 Sep. 2024].

Cunningham, S. (2021). Patricia Gregory: 'We never imagined girls would be paid to play football'. [online] inews.co.uk. Available at: https://inews.co.uk/sport/football/patricia-gregory-womens-football-ban-fa-cup-final-1971-white-ribbon-991917 [Accessed 20 Sep. 2024].

Dent, M. (2015). Thirty Years Before Abby Wambach was Even Born, These Women Pioneered Soccer in America. [online] Slate Magazine. Available at: https://slate.com/culture/2015/06/women-s-world-cup-2015 -before-any-team-usa-members-were-even-born-these-women-started-the-first-women-s-soccer-league-in-america.html [Accessed 20 Sep. 2024].

Dure, B. (2022). 50 years of Title IX: the US law that attempted to make sports equal. [online] The Guardian. Available at: https://www.theguardian.com/sport/2022/jun/23/50-years-of-title-ix-the-us-law-that-attempted-to-make-sports-equal [Accessed 20 Sep. 2024].

Englandfootballonline.com. (2024). England Matches - The England Women's Football Team 1970-90. [online] Available at: http://www.englandfootballonline.com/matchrsl/MatchRslTmWompg1.html [Accessed 20 Sep. 2024].

Exploring Trafford's Heritage. (n.d.). WFA CUP FINAL: 1989 Women's Football in Trafford   Exploring Trafford's Heritage. [online] Available at:

https://exploringtraffordsheritage.omeka.net/exhibits/show/traff
ordwomensfootball/1989wfacupfinal [Accessed 20 Sep. 2024].

Faller, H. (2021). The Forgotten Pioneers: International Women's
Football in the Interwar Period Part 2 | Playing Pasts. [online]
Playingpasts.co.uk. Available at:
https://www.playingpasts.co.uk/articles/football/the-forgotten-
pioneers-international-womens-football-in-the-interwar-period-p
art-2/ [Accessed 20 Sep. 2024].

FIFA.com, archives. (n.d.). Women's World Cup 1991 Technical
Report. [online] Available at:
https://web.archive.org/web/20111227003624/http://www.fifa.
com/mm/document/afdeveloping/technicaldevp/50/08/19/ww
c%5f91%5ftr%5fpart2%5f260.pdf [Accessed 20 Sep. 2024].

Football Australia (2021). History of Women's Football in
Australia. [online] Football Australia. Available at:
https://www.footballaustralia.com.au/history-womens-football-
australia [Accessed 20 Sep. 2024].

Frejfors, T. (2013). Women's EURO ticket sales record broken.
[online] UEFA.com. Available at:
https://www.uefa.com/news/020b-0e1426ecee1b-9cbe054f0fad-
1000--women-s-euro-ticket-sales-record-broken/ [Accessed 20
Sep. 2024].

Garin, E., Hansson, O. and Morrison, N. (2021). Coppa Europa
per Nazioni (Women) 1969. [online] Rsssf.org. Available at:
https://www.rsssf.org/tablese/eur-women69.html [Accessed 20
Sep. 2024].

Garin, E., Hansson, O., Morrison, N. and Stokkermans, K. (2021). Coppa del Mondo (Women) 1970. [online] Rsssf.org. Available at: https://www.rsssf.org/tablesm/mondo-women70.html [Accessed 20 Sep. 2024].

Gilles Dhers (2019). Fémina sport : aux sources du foot des femmes en France. [online] Libération. Available at: https://www.liberation.fr/sports/2019/06/10/femina-sport-aux-sources-du-foot-des-femmes-en-france_1732338/ [Accessed 20 Sep. 2024].

Hall, R. (2022). 'A cultural moment': what Bend It Like Beckham meant for UK women's football. [online] the Guardian. Available at: https://www.theguardian.com/football/2022/apr/12/a-cultural-moment-what-bend-it-like-beckham-meant-for-uk-womens-football [Accessed 20 Sep. 2024].

Harpur, C. (2022). Banned, ignored... adored: How England fought to become women's Euro 2022 champions. [online] The Athletic. Available at: https://www.nytimes.com/athletic/3464251/2022/07/31/england-women-euro-2022/?access_token=12062815&redirected=1 [Accessed 20 Sep. 2024].

Heritage Doncaster. (n.d.). Gillian Coulthard MBE. [online] Available at: https://www.heritagedoncaster.org.uk/projects/herstory/exploreherstory/gillian-coultard/# [Accessed 20 Sep. 2024].

History of the Women's Football Association. (2018). Carol Thomas (née McCune). [online] Available at: https://wfahistory.wordpress.com/in-their-own-words/carol-thomas/ [Accessed 20 Sep. 2024].

Hoffmann, E. and Nendza, J. (2007). Women's Football During the Ban. [online] bpb.de. Available at: https://web.archive.org/web/20220218220314/https://www.bpb.de/themen/sport/graue-spielzeit/65065/damenfussball-in-der-verbotszeit/ [Accessed 20 Sep. 2024].

Hong, F. and Mangan, J. eds., (2004). Soccer, Women, Sexual Liberation. 1st ed. [online] Google Books. London, Portland Oregon: Frank Cass Publishers. Available at: https://books.google.co.uk/books?id=Ac1cwirO44oC&q=women%27s+soccer+in+canada&pg=PA30&redir_esc=y#v=snippet&q=women [Accessed 20 Sep. 2024].

inside.fifa.com. (2023). New payment model guarantees support for every FIFA Women's World Cup 2023TM team and player. [online] Available at: https://inside.fifa.com/tournaments/womens/womensworldcup/australia-new-zealand2023/media-releases/new-payment-model-guarantees-support-for-every-fifa-womens-world-cup-2023-tm [Accessed 20 Sep. 2024].

Jessica Gregory and Iglikowski-Broad, V. (2023). The National Archives: History's Lionesses: The British Ladies Football Team and the Beautiful Game in 1895. [online] The National Archives.

doi:https://blog.nationalarchives.gov.uk/historys-lionesses/#retu rn-note-63411-8[Accessed 20 Sep. 2024].

Kobzar, E. (2023). Elsie Cook's football revolution is huge departure from days of borrowing strips and begging for boots. [online] Daily Record. Available at: https://www.dailyrecord.co.uk/ayrshire/elsie-cooks-football-revo lution-huge-29393707 [Accessed 20 Sep. 2024].

Lacey-Hatton, J. (2023). Arsenal star rips into Ballon d'Or organisers amid Novak Djokovic criticism and schedule issue. [online] Mirror. Available at: https://www.mirror.co.uk/sport/football/news/arsenal-jen-beatt ie-ballon-dor-31327634 [Accessed 20 Sep. 2024].

Leigh, M.H. and Bonin, T.M. (1977). The Pioneering Role Of Madame Alice Milliat and the FSFI in Establishing International Trade and Field Competition for Women. Journal of Sport History, [online] 4(1), pp.72–83. Available at: https://www.jstor.org/stable/43611530 [Accessed 20 Sep. 2024].

Leighton, T. (2009). FA boosts England's women's team with central contracts. [online] the Guardian. Available at: https://www.theguardian.com/football/2009/may/14/womens-f ootball-central-contracts-fa-england [Accessed 20 Sep. 2024].

Lopez, S. (1997). Women on the ball : a guide to women's football. London: Scarlet Press.

Malone, R. (2022). The hidden history of women's football in England. [online] Sports Gazette. Available at:

https://sportsgazette.co.uk/the-hidden-history-of-womens-fo
otball-in-england/ [Accessed 20 Sep. 2024].

Mitchell, K. (2021). The history of the Canadian women's
soccer team: From men's hand-me-downs to gold-medal game.
National Post. [online] 5 Aug. Available at:
https://nationalpost.com/sports/olympics/the-history-of-the-
canadian-womens-soccer-team-from-mens-hand-me-downs-t
o-gold-medal-game [Accessed 20 Sep. 2024].

Mzizi, S. (2023). By the Numbers: Why the 2023 FIFA
Women's World Cup Was a Successful Project. [online]
ITonlinelearning. Available at:
https://www.itonlinelearning.com/blog/by-the-numbers-wh
y-the-2023-fifa-womens-world-cup-was-a-successful-project/
[Accessed 20 Sep. 2024].

National Football Museum. (n.d.). Sheila Parker Hall of Fame
profile. [online] Available at:
https://nationalfootballmuseum.com/halloffame/sheila-parke
r/ [Accessed 20 Sep. 2024].

Newsham, G. (n.d.). KICKING OFF.
[online] www.dickkerrladies.com. Available at:
https://www.dickkerrladies.com/kicking-off [Accessed 20 Sep.
2024].

Newsham, G.J. (1988). In a league of their own! The Dick,
Kerr Ladies' Football Club. Gail J Newsham & Paragon
Publishing.

Nzfootball.co.nz. (2017). Ford Football
Ferns - History. [online] Available
at: https://www.nzfootball.co.nz/history/football-ferns
[Accessed 20 Sep. 2024].

Ovedie Skogvang, B. (2007). The Historical Development of
Women's football in Norway: From 'Show Games' to
International Successes. In: J. Magee, J. Caudwell, K. Liston
and S. Scraton, eds., Women, Football, and Europe: Histories,
Equity and Experiences. [online] Meyer & Meyer Sport,
pp.41–54. Available at:
https://www.researchgate.net/publication/315840483_The_
Historical_Development_of_Women%27s_football_in_Nor
way_From_%27Show_Games%27_to_International_Success
es [Accessed 20 Sep. 2024].

Pfeiffer, M. (2020). DFB: 50 Jahre nach Ende des Verbots des
Frauenfußballs. [online] SPORT1. Available at:
https://www.sport1.de/news/fussball/2020/10/deutscher-fus
sball-bund-50-jahre-frauenfussball-das-falsche-jubilaeum
[Accessed 20 Sep. 2024].

Pieper, L. (2015). The Beleaguered History of the Women's
World Cup. [online] Sport in American History. Available at:
https://ussporthistory.com/2015/07/02/the-beleaguered-hist
ory-of-the-womens-world-cup/ [Accessed 20 Sep. 2024].

Rangers.co.uk. (2023). Margaret McAulay Meets Rangers Squad.
[online] Available at:
https://www.rangers.co.uk/article/margaret-mcaulay-meets-rang

ers-squad/3mNCLgPDDmTcMWrZnTrbcc [Accessed 20 Sep. 2024].

Rich, T. (2013). Relegation scandal takes toll on Doncaster Rovers Belles. [online] Independent. Available at: https://www.independent.co.uk/sport/football/news/relegation-scandal-takes-toll-on-doncaster-rovers-belles-8650856.html [Accessed 20 Sep. 2024].

Rinaldi, G. (2023). Lady Florence Dixie: The aristocrat who fought for women's football. BBC News. [online] 23 Jul. Available at: https://www.bbc.co.uk/news/uk-scotland-south-scotland-66232 240 [Accessed 20 Sep. 2024].

Saffer, P. (2013). Sixth maybe the best for Germany. [online] UEFA.com. Available at: https://www.uefa.com/news/0252-0ce447fd8df5-ab59a1b6e0b1 -1000--sixth-maybe-the-best-for-germany/ [Accessed 20 Sep. 2024].

Scottish Football Museum. (2019). The 1972 Women's Scotland v. England Game. [online] Available at: https://www.scottishfootballmuseum.org.uk/news/first-womens -international-match-1972/#:~:text=The%20Scottish%20side%2 0was%20managed [Accessed 20 Sep. 2024].

Shopland, N. (2023). The roots of women's football in Wales. [online] Nation.Cymru. Available at: https://nation.cymru/culture/the-roots-of-womens-football-in-wales/ [Accessed 20 Sep. 2024].

Skillen, F., Byrne, H., Carrier, J. and James, G. (2022). 'The Game of Football Is Quite Unsuitable for Females and Ought Not to Be encouraged': a Comparative Analysis of the 1921 English Football Association Ban on women's Football in Britain and Ireland. Sport in History, [online] 42(1), pp.1–27. doi:https://doi.org/10.1080/17460263.2021.2025415[Accessed 20 Sep. 2024].

Smith, F. (2022). 'It's brilliant the England Women's players of today still remember the 1972 team'. [online] https://www.englandfootball.com. Available at: https://www.englandfootball.com/articles/2022/Nov/18/england-women-jeannie-allott-interview-20221118 [Accessed 20 Sep. 2024].

Sportingintelligence.com. (2011). REVEALED: Official English football wage figures for the past 25 years | Sporting Intelligence. [online] Available at: https://www.sportingintelligence.com/2011/10/30/revealed-official-english-football-wage-figures-for-the-past-25-years-301002/#:~:text=In%202009%2D10%2C%20the%20average [Accessed 20 Sep. 2024].

Statista. (2023). Women's World Cup total attendance 2023 | Statista. [online] Available at: https://www.statista.com/statistics/1386762/womens-world-cup-total-attendance/#:~:text=Total%20attendance%20at%20the%20Women [Accessed 20 Sep. 2024].

Szerovay, M., Nevala, A. and Itkonen, H. eds., (2023). Football in the Nordic Countries. London: Routledge Taylor & Francis Group.

The Football Association (2020). Manchester FA. [online] www.manchesterfa.com. Available at: https://www.manchesterfa.com/news/2020/mar/08/manchester-corinthians-ladies [Accessed 20 Sep. 2024].

The Football Association (2022). Learn more about the heritage of women's football in Milton Keynes. [online] www.thefa.com. Available at: https://www.thefa.com/competitions/uefa-womens-euro-2022/heritage/milton-keynes-heritage [Accessed 20 Sep. 2024].

Tomlinson, A. (2010). A Dictionary of Sports Studies. [online] Google Books, Oxford: Oxford University Press, p.490. Available at: https://books.google.co.uk/books?id=r_Ujf9-TmBUC&lpg=PA490&dq=british%20ladies%20football%20team&pg=PA490#v=onepage&q=british%20ladies%20football%20team&f=false [Accessed 20 Sep. 2024].

Turner, K. (2017). Scrapbooking: Preserving the stories of Manchester's Corinthian Ladies. [online] Unlocking the hidden history of women's football. Available at: https://unlockingthehiddenhistory.wordpress.com/2017/08/14/scrapbooking-an-insight-into-manchesters-corinthian-ladies/ [Accessed 20 Sep. 2024].

UEFA.com (2005). 2005: Official approval for EURO success. [online] UEFA.com. Available at: https://www.uefa.com/news/01aa-0e1098d51808-b57593af5 03a-1000--2005-official-approval-for-euro-success/ [Accessed 20 Sep. 2024].

UEFA.com (2022). How the UEFA Women's EURO was born. [online] UEFA.com. Available at: https://www.uefa.com/womenseuro/news/026e-1394543e97 e3-cdbd4893092f-1000--how-the-uefa-women-s-euro-was-bo rn/ [Accessed 20 Sep. 2024].

UEFA.com (2022). UEFA Women's EURO 2022 positive impact and future legacy revealed in post-tournament flash report | Inside UEFA. [online] UEFA.com. Available at: https://www.uefa.com/insideuefa/news/027a-164415be92b2 -36f88ae7c9ec-1000--uefa-women-s-euro-2022-positive-impa ct-and-future-legacy-rev/ [Accessed 20 Sep. 2024].

UEFA.com (2023). Women's Champions League attendances still surging upward. [online] UEFA.com. Available at: https://www.uefa.com/womenschampionsleague/news/0281 -17ec3944f311-325d53d00720-1000--women-s-champions-le ague-attendances-still-surging-upward/ [Accessed 20 Sep. 2024].

Williams, J. (n.d.). Women's Football during the First World War. [online] Football and the First World War. Available at: https://www.footballandthefirstworldwar.org/womens-footb all-first-world-war/ [Accessed 20 Sep. 2024].

Wilson, B. (2018). Mexico 1971: When women's football hit the big time. BBC News. [online] 7 Dec. Available at: https://www.bbc.co.uk/news/business-46149887 [Accessed 20 Sep. 2024].

Women's Football Archive. (2014). Portopia '81 – England women tour Japan. [online] Available at: https://womensfootballarchive.org/2014/07/19/portopia-81-england-women-tour-japan/ [Accessed 20 Sep. 2024].

wslhalloffame.thefa.com. (n.d.). A Moment in Women's Football History. [online] Available at: https://wslhalloffame.thefa.com/history [Accessed 20 Sep. 2024].

www.common-goal.org. (n.d.). 1971 Unoffical World Cup - Common Goal. [online] Available at: https://www.common-goal.org/Stories/1971-Unoffical-World-Cup2022-08-19 [Accessed 20 Sep. 2024].

www.european-football-statistics.co.uk. (2024). History of English Football. League attendance. [online] Available at: https://www.european-football-statistics.co.uk/attn/nav/attnengleague.htm [Accessed 20 Sep. 2024].

www.stff.se. (n.d.). Damfotbollen står stark – men mycket finns att göra - Stockholm. [online] Available at: https://www.stff.se/om-oss/historia/ann-jansson-blev-historisk-malskytt/[Accessed 20 Sep. 2024].

Acknowledgements

I'd like to thank Carol Thomas, Rachel Brown-Finnis, Issy Pollard, and Gurinder Chadha for sharing their time and experiences during the research for this book. It was an absolute pleasure hearing your stories.

I'd also like to thank Helen Rowe-Willcocks for writing such a generous foreword and for giving me the opportunity to write for *The Women's Football Magazine*.

Thank you to my beta readers, Katie Scott and Tanita Fernandes. Your comments and encouragement have improved this book and kept me going whenever I doubted myself. Your time and energy is hugely appreciated.

Thanks also to my husband for putting up with the hours I've spent tapping away at my keyboard, and to my son for putting up with my cries of "not now" when he's asking for more game time on his Switch.

About the author

Clare McEwen fell in love with football as a girl in the 1980s. She spent countless hours with a ball at her feet but wasn't allowed to play in a team (although she did briefly try to start her own!).

Watching the Lionesses play at Wembley decades later brought up a bucketload of emotions. Driven by these emotions and a need to understand the game's hidden history, she set out on a journey to uncover the stories of the women who made it possible.

Clare writes for *The Women's Football Magazine* and is an experienced epidemiology researcher at the University of Oxford. In her free time, she coaches her son's Under-13s football team, as yet, fairly unsuccessfully.

www.ingramcontent.com/pod-product-compliance
Ingram Content Group UK Ltd.
Pitfield, Milton Keynes, MK11 3LW, UK
UKHW021026130225
455029UK00009B/94